D1179970

THE VINDICATION OF LIBERAL THEOLOGY

OTHER BOOKS BY THE SAME AUTHOR

One Great Ground of Hope: Christian Missions and Christian Unity

Spirit, Son and Father

God in Education

Life's Meaning: The Why and How of Christian Living

World Christianity: Yesterday, Today and Tomorrow

They Found the Church There

East Indies Discoveries

What IS the Church Doing?

Reality and Religion (HAZEN SERIES)

Methodism's World Mission

For the Healing of the Nations: Impressions of Christianity Around the World

God in These Times

The Plain Man Seeks for God

In Quest of Life's Meaning

EDITED BY HENRY P. VAN DUSEN

Christianity on the March

The Spiritual Legacy of John Foster Dulles

The Library of Christian Classics (WITH JOHN T. MCNEILL AND JOHN BAILLIE)

The Christian Answer

Liberal Theology: An Appraisal (WITH DAVID E. ROBERTS)

Church and State in the Modern World

The Church Through Half a Century (WITH SAMUEL MCCREA CAVERT)

Ventures in Belief

The Story of Jesus (WITH THOMAS W. GRAHAM)

THE VINDICATION *of* LIBERAL THEOLOGY

A Tract for the Times

by

HENRY P. VAN DUSEN

Based upon

The Eugene William Lyman Memorial Lecture

Sweet Briar College

Charles Scribner's Sons, New York

THIS BOOK PUBLISHED SIMULTANEOUSLY IN THE
UNITED STATES OF AMERICA AND IN CANADA—
COPYRIGHT UNDER THE BERNE CONVENTION

A-4.63[V]

PRINTED IN THE UNITED STATES OF AMERICA

LIBRARY OF CONGRESS CATALOG CARD NUMBER 63-12024

To My Colleagues

of the Faculty of
UNION THEOLOGICAL SEMINARY

1926–1963

with admiration, gratitude
and enduring affection.

PREFACE

When I was invited to give the EUGENE WILLIAM LYMAN MEMORIAL LECTURE at Sweet Briar College in the autumn of 1962, only one topic suggested itself as appropriate to the occasion. If it were to be a suitable tribute to the man in whose honor the lectureship had been established, it must treat of Liberal Theology.

Just twenty years earlier, two former students of Dr. Lyman, at that time his junior colleagues on the Faculty of Union Theological Seminary in New York, had undertaken to enlist a group of his admirers in preparing a collection of "Essays in Honor of Eugene William Lyman" on his retirement from active teaching at Union. What should be the symposium's title, its *motif,* the connecting-thread of its fifteen chapters? The answer to that question was inescapable. The volume was to bear the dedication:

To
EUGENE WILLIAM LYMAN
Liberal Christian Thinker.

Clearly, its contents must focus upon Liberal Theology. But at that moment, "Liberal Theology" was all too evidently on the defensive; many would have said it was discredited, some that it was disgraced, not a few that it was already demised, awaiting only a proper interment.

Ten years before, as a brash young theologian aged 32, I had myself written a little article under the caption "The Sickness of Liberal Religion" which set down the thesis: "Possibly the most certain fact in the present baffling religious situation is the ill-health of liberal Christianity."[1] I mention this, not because of any intrinsic merit in the article, but to indicate that the author of this essay was not impervious to or unaffected by the prevailing "retreat from Liberalism." Two years after that, another of Dr. Lyman's former pupils and assistants who has won recognition across the years for an exceptionally fair and judicious as well as acute insight, Dr. John C. Bennett, posed the question: *"After Liberalism—What?"*[2] with this opening declaration: "The most important fact about contemporary American theology is the disintegration of liberalism. Disintegration may seem too strong a word, but I am using it quite literally." And in 1939, one of the ablest and weightiest Christian thinkers of his generation, Professor Robert L. Calhoun of Yale, in a *Christian Century* series on "How My Mind Has Changed in the Past Decade" had titled his *confessio fidei:* "A Liberal Bandaged but Unbowed."[3]

Such was the atmosphere in which this group of friends proposed to pay tribute to Eugene Lyman as "Liberal Christian Thinker."

The older of the two Editors proposed as the book's title: "Liberal Theology: A Vindication." But his colleague, fifteen years younger, could not, with good conscience, permit his name to sponsor a "vindication." After considerable discussion, a neutral characterization was agreed upon: "Liberal Theology: An Appraisal."[4] Thus the book was christened.

Now, two decades later, the senior of the two Editors was invited

1. In *The World Tomorrow,* August 1931, pp. 256–59.
2. In *The Christian Century,* November 3, 1933, pp. 1403–1406.
3. *The Christian Century,* May 31, 1939.
4. *Liberal Theology: An Appraisal,* ed. D. E. Roberts and H. P. Van Dusen. Scribners, 1942.

to Sweet Briar College, so intimately and affectionately associated with Dr. Lyman's last years, on a Lectureship bearing his name. This time, there was no impediment in phrasing of theme. Moreover, there is virtue in forthrightness with one's audience, in confessing at the outset one's convictions, rather than disguising them with subtleties and circumlocutions, only to have them unmasked at the end. Hence the title of the Lyman Memorial Lecture for 1962, and of this book which is a radical recasting and substantial expansion of the lecture as originally prepared and given.

The two decades which have intervened since the volume of tribute to Dr. Lyman have witnessed no marked change in the theological atmosphere which then obtained, no alleviation of the discredit of Liberal Theology. The "existential situation" to which these pages are addressed is very similar to that in 1942. Nevertheless, there is evidence that the time is ripe for a "reappraisal." Indeed, after the lecture for Sweet Briar was virtually completed in first draft, there came into my hands by all odds the most thorough and able examination of Liberal Theology yet written, Dr. Kenneth Cauthen's *The Impact of American Religious Liberalism*.[5] In revising the lecture for publication, I have made extensive reference to this book, both its exposition and its critique.

Since my diagnosis of the "sickness" of liberal religion more than thirty years ago, I have written much, in a variety of contexts, on the underlying issues and the central convictions of Liberal Theology. Some of these writings have never been published; virtually all of the others have long been out of print. Since this small work is in the nature of a precis of some four decades' reflection on its theme, where the earlier discussions are still relevant and valid I have not hesitated to incorporate here sentences and occasional sections from them. As indispensable context for an understanding of the rise and

5. Harper and Row, 1962.

character of Liberal Theology, there is appended an essay on "The Farther Background: Theology in the Nineteenth Century." [6]

Doubtless, this book shows the circumstances of its composition. The final draft has been completed in hours snatched from routine tasks. This is said not by way of excuse; every author must take full responsibility for the inadequacies of his writing. Rather, in the hope that it may encourage readers, whether friends or critics, to distinguish between *substance* and *form of presentation*. The latter may, at some points, suggest haste or pressure or imbalance. The *substance* of the argument, however, represents the distillation of forty years of reflection upon what is to me the pivotal issue of Christian Faith —the significance of Jesus Christ—and the validity and adequacy of Liberal Theology's interpretation of that Reality.

* * * * *

To President Anne Gary Pannell and the Faculty of Sweet Briar College for the invitation to deliver the Lyman Memorial Lecture in 1962, to the Faculty and students of Sweet Briar for a most gracious welcome, eager attention and generous response, and especially to Dr. Mary Ely Lyman who, in Dr. Pannell's absence, presided at the lecture, urged its publication and has given the original text the benefit of discerning comment, I am greatly indebted. I am also grateful to Dr. Morgan P. Noyes who has read the entire manuscript with meticulous attention and has offered many suggestions for improvement, and to my two senior colleagues in New Testament, Dr. John Knox and Dr. W. D. Davies, who have scrutinized the climactic chapter on "THE DECISIVE ISSUE: THE CENTRALITY AND AUTHORITY OF JESUS CHRIST," although I have not been able, at all points, to incorporate the alterations which they have proposed.

Special thanks are also due a corps of ever-willing secretaries who have added to their regular duties the tedious task of copying, re-

6. See pp. 155 ff.

copying and correction—Mrs. Harold C. Letts and her colleagues, Miss Rae Beth Parrott and Mrs. Alistair Kee. No record of indebtedness, however cursory, would be complete without an expression of special appreciation to my close friend and collaborator in publishing for more than thirty years, Mr. William L. Savage of Scribners, who has not only characteristically given the text and proof his personal supervision at each successive stage but has pressed the book through to publication in record time to fulfill a particular deadline which I had proposed.

A word about the dedication. I had hoped, on retiring from the Faculty of Union Seminary, to present those who have been associated with me over nearly forty years with a more substantial contribution to our common enterprise of interpreting Christian Faith to the minds of today; but the demands of routine responsibilities have prevented the fulfillment of that hope. My hesitancy over the dedication is all the greater because I realize that, to a number of my present colleagues, some of the views so frankly and forcefully set forth are not altogether congenial. They will recognize, however, that these convictions have not been newly formed but have controlled my thinking across the years, though their expression may have been muted! In any event, this small book, attempting to deal with what I believe to be the *central* issue of our work together, is offered to them as a token of affection and regard—an earnest, but not a promise, of a more worthy tribute.

H. P. V. D.

UNION THEOLOGICAL SEMINARY,
NEW YORK,
APRIL 27, 1963

CONTENTS

* * * * *

CHAPTER ONE

INTRODUCTION

1. THE INTENTION OF THE INQUIRY

2. IS THERE A "LIBERAL THEOLOGY"?

CHAPTER ONE

INTRODUCTION

1. THE INTENTION OF THE INQUIRY

The title of this book defines its intention. It makes bold to attempt a "vindication of Liberal Theology."

It will seek to establish three contentions:

First. There is a distinguishable body of belief, a definable position, which may properly be designated "Liberal Theology."

Second. This "Liberal Theology" was, in its origin and initial formulation, something *genuinely new* in the pilgrimage of Christian Faith down the ages—in the current phrase, something of a "breakthrough"; not wholly "new" in spirit or outlook to be sure, but new, unprecedented, precisely in its specific content of conviction.

Third. Here is the heart of the matter: that "Liberal Theology," with all of the inadequacies which mark every Theology and despite the distortions which infect any Theology from the intellectual and cultural milieu of the Age of its birth, was—and is—the least inadequate, most credible and cogent interpretation of Christian Faith in the nineteen centuries of its history. A daring contention—that, in the view of many! Nevertheless, it is advanced in all seriousness.

2. IS THERE A "LIBERAL THEOLOGY"?

At the outset, we must face the query: *Is there any such thing as "Liberal Theology,"* "a distinguishable body of belief, a definable position"?

Here, we confront a divided voice among "liberal" Christians themselves. Many who gladly confess themselves "liberals in theology" have been at pains to deny that "Liberalism" *is* a Theology. Rather, they maintain, it is an "outlook," an "approach," a "point of view," a "spirit"—the "liberal spirit" in Theology. Thus, my revered teacher and predecessor, Dr. Henry Sloane Coffin:

> "By 'liberalism' is meant that spirit which reveres truth supremely, and therefore craves freedom to ascertain, to discuss, to publish, and to pursue that which is believed to be true, and seeks fellowship in its discovery." [1]

Assuredly that *is* the outlook which animates theological liberals, which sets them on their quest and guides them throughout their course—a "spirit" which makes liberalism in Theology close kin to liberalism in science, in politics, in social reform. But is that all? It is my contention that the Liberal mind's fidelity to truth has led to distinctive, identifiable theological conclusions, and that it is the latter which constitute "Liberal Theology." In fact, Liberal Theology is *both* a "spirit" *and* a body of "conviction." This dual nature becomes apparent the moment we examine its origins.

1. "Can Liberalism Survive?" in *Religion in Life,* Spring Issue, 1935, p. 194. This was always a matter of friendly difference between Dr. Coffin and myself.

CHAPTER TWO

THE ANCESTRY OF LIBERAL THEOLOGY

1. THE OUTLOOK OF THE "MODERN MIND"

a. Fidelity to Truth

b. Deference to Science and the Historical Movement

c. Tentativeness as to Metaphysical Certainty

d. The Assumption of Continuity

2. RELIGIOUS EVANGELICALISM

a. The Authority of Christian Experience

b. The Centrality of Jesus Christ

c. Loyalty to the Historic Faith

d. Moral and Social Compassion and Dedication

CHAPTER TWO

THE ANCESTRY OF LIBERAL THEOLOGY[1]

At birth, Liberal Theology was the child of two parents, as every proper child should be: on the one hand, the *intellectual outlook* of the late nineteenth and early twentieth centuries, the Age in which it arose; on the other hand, the *religious resurgence* of that same Period. Each parent bequeathed to their child two dominant endowments; these, in turn, found expression in four major characteristics from each parent.

If I may press the metaphor, one parent was, appropriately, more masculine in temper; the other, more feminine. The first gave to Liberal Theology its *intellectual perspective*—its openness to new truth; its boldness, its venturesomeness, sometimes its bravado; its critical-mindedness; its self-confidence, perhaps overconfidence; its contemporaneity—all typical characteristics of the masculine mind; and also, its *basic theoretical assumption*. The second gave to Liberal Theology its *spiritual vitality and power*—its awareness that life is

1. Any adequate consideration of the sources of Liberal Theology must search for them in the longer perspective of the development of philosophical and theological thought through the nineteenth century. This is sketched in a supplementary essay on "The Farther Background," pp. 155ff.

more than mind, and so must religion be; its sense of linkage with the past, of the wisdom of the Ages; its contagious spirituality and its moral consciousness, lofty ideals, demanding obligations—all distinctive qualities of the feminine spirit; and also its *central and regnant positive conviction,* the fulcrum upon which it was securely based.

As might have been expected, the children of this marriage were not one but several. So there has been not a single Liberal Theology but many. They differed mainly in the degree of indebtedness to one or the other parent. Just here arises confusion in classification, a confusion of complexity, and the difficulty of arriving at any agreed definition of Liberal Theology. As we would expect, some of the progeny were more influenced by the male parent, attaching primary importance to his intellectual outlook and presuppositions; others were more determined by the female parent, leaning heavily on her gift of vibrant spiritual experience, centering in a rediscovery of Jesus Christ. The most authentic Liberal Theology recognized and confessed its debtorship to *both* parents, and sought to hold its dual heritage in a true, but never easy, union.[2]

Thus, Liberal Theology is, and has always been, something of a "bridge-theology"—one foot firmly planted upon Modern Thought, the other deeply rooted within Christian experience. But, to continue the figure, the footings of this suspension bridge were not immutably anchored at either end. "Modern Thought" often seems more like shifting sands, and the Modern Mind erected upon it like a swinging stanchion, as Paul described the Modern Mind of his day, "tossed to and fro and swayed by every wind of doctrine" ("whirled about by every fresh gust of teaching").[3] And, "Christian experience" has

2. In an essay written a quarter of a century ago on "The Liberal Movement in Theology," I distinguished four principal types. Cf. *The Church Through Half A Century,* Scribners, 1936, pp. 70–72.

3. Ephesians 4:14.

offered hardly more secure foundation, fluctuating as though on a flowing and ebbing tide. Small wonder that the bridge which sought to link these two supports should seem insecure, precarious, leaning upon first one and then the other ever-changing base.

To return to our earlier and more appropriate metaphor, Liberal Theology has sought to be true to both its parents, radically different and contrasted in their inner natures. In its adolescent years, it may be likened to a precocious youth within a family who tries to hold together the father, a highly sophisticated and sceptical man-of-the-world, and the mother, a deeply devout and dedicated woman-of-faith. Of many of the earlier evangelical liberal teachers and preachers it was said: "He thinks like a Modernist but prays like a Fundamentalist." In its later maturity, this dual heritage continues to induce inner strain and the external appearance of insecurity and inconsistency, as the Evangelical Liberal is dominated by first one and then the other set of inherited characteristics.

From the pressures of that tension, one might seek release in one of three ways. One might surrender standing-ground upon Christian tradition and traditional Christian experience, give oneself wholly to the point-of-view, assumptions and dogmas of "Modern Thought," take up a position there, and then seek to reclaim as much as possible of historic Christian Faith; that is the essence of "Modernism" and should be clearly and sharply distinguished from "Liberalism" which is too often confused with "Modernism."[4] Alternatively, one might disavow much of the widely accepted structure of "Modern Thought," recover and reaffirm historic Christian Faith, and then seek to incorporate as much as possible of the new truth; that, in essence, is "Neo-Orthodoxy." But there is a third possibility: to acknowledge debtor-

4. One of the embarrassments of authentic Liberal Theology is that the most vocal and militant apologists for Liberalism are so often more correctly identified as Modernists.

ship to *both* parents, to refuse the easier and more comfortable resolution of the tension by disavowal of one or the other, to insist upon the partial but incomplete truth of each, to seek to purge each legacy of its inadequacies—Modern Thought of its exaggerated aberrations, Christian Tradition of its outmoded superstitions—and declare a conviction, at once credible to the Mind of Today and yet in unmistakable and unchallengeable continuity with *true* Christian Faith, i.e. the faith of Jesus of Nazareth. *This* is authentic Evangelical Liberalism.[5]

The most comprehensive and adequate account and critique of Liberal Theology has appeared while this essay was in preparation.[6] Its author, a young professor of theology in Crozer Seminary, Dr. Kenneth Cauthen, follows a similar classification. He cites a phrase from Dr. Harry Emerson Fosdick's autobiography, that the central aim of Liberal Theology was to make it possible for a man "to be both an intelligent modern and a serious Christian,"[7] and identifies two basic types of liberalism—"Evangelical Liberalism"[8] and "Modernistic Liberalism." He suggests that "The evangelical liberals can appropriately be thought of as 'serious Christians' who were searching for a theology which could be believed by 'intelligent moderns' " while "The modernistic liberals can best be thought of as 'intelligent mod-

5. The Editors of the most distinguished shelf of theological writings in our day, *The Library of Constructive Theology,* declare that "Nothing less is required than a candid, courageous, and well-informed effort to think out anew, in the light of modern knowledge, the foundation affirmations of our common Christianity," and affirm that "the starting-point of reconstruction" must be "the value and validity of religious experience." "General Introduction" to the Series.

6. Kenneth Cauthen, *The Impact of American Religious Liberalism,* Harper and Row, 1962.

7. *The Living of These Days,* Harper, 1956, p. vii.

8. Dr. Henry Sloane Coffin again spoke for many Liberal colleagues in his oft-reiterated insistence that the order of the two terms should be reversed, that the only proper designation for Liberal Theology is "Liberal Evangelicalism." See, below, p. 38.

erns' who nevertheless wished to be thought of as 'serious Christians' in some real sense." [9] Dr. Cauthen distinguishes two sub-types in each group: "ethical-social liberals" and "metaphysical liberals" among evangelicals, and "ethical-social" and "empirical" modernistic liberals.[10] He further recognizes that, on either side of all liberals, whether "evangelical" or "modernistic," have stood two other major groups in contemporary theology: "Fundamentalists and conservatives who were primarily interested in being 'serious Christians' " without attempting to be "intelligent moderns" and "Humanists who were interested only in being 'intelligent moderns' and rejected Christianity outright." [11]

Once again, as might have been foreseen, and as is so often the case in human families, each parent bequeathed to each child both good and evil—some things which were true, priceless, permanently valid; some things which were inadequate, ephemeral, of transient worth.

From the vast and intricate complex of this dual inheritance, at the risk of undue simplification and omission of what some may consider important, we shall identify four contributions from each parent.

I. THE OUTLOOK OF THE "MODERN MIND"

a. Fidelity to Truth

To its *masculine* parent—the intellectual outlook of the Modern Age—Liberal Theology owed, above everything else, its *devotion to truth,* its fearless openness to new truth, its insistence upon bringing

9. Cauthen, *op. cit.,* pp. 27, 29. Dr. Cauthen states that, in this basic classification, he is following an earlier analysis by me (p. 260).

10. *Ibid.,* p. 33.

11. *Ibid.,* pp. 30–32.

the heritage of the past—Christian tradition, historic theology, even Christian origins and the Bible—under the judgment of new and authentic knowledge, to the test of Truth. We have already quoted Dr. Coffin. In the volume of essays honoring Dr. Eugene W. Lyman on his retirement in 1942, he again insisted: "The characteristic of a liberal is his unrestrained response to truth, wherever it encounters him." [12] In this insistence, Dr. Coffin spoke for his fellow-liberals; the same note rings like a refrain through all advocacies of Liberal Theology.

So, Dr. William Pierson Merrill defined as the first mark of a "liberal Christian": "one who keeps an open mind toward truth. . . . That is to say, he refuses to admit to himself that *any* question is ever irrevocably settled." [13] And Professor William Ernest Hocking, attempting a "definition" of Liberalism for the symposium in tribute to Dr. Lyman, declared: "The social function of the liberal, i.e. he who lives as a free man should and can live, is to expand, explore, and experiment, trying leads here and there, which may be useless, on the chance that among them something new and important may be lighted upon." [14]

How great a release from intellectual bondage this basic principle —fidelity to truth rather than to tradition—brought to eager young minds of an earlier day, it is difficult for a generation which has never known any other intellectual climate to comprehend. Only those who have lived in a world dominated by theological obscurantism, or its aftermath, can fully appreciate the liberation of that devotion.

The primary motivation of this basic liberal principle—loyalty to truth—is, of course, intellectual honesty, fundamental personal integrity.

12. *Liberal Theology: An Appraisal,* p. 223.

13. *Liberal Christianity,* Macmillan, 1925, p. 27.

14. *Liberal Theology: An Appraisal,* p. 47.

Hardly less compelling, however, is the motive which dominates the liberal theologian as he looks out upon and confronts the world in which he dwells. As Dr. John C. Bennett has said: "Underlying the specific convictions of liberals there is the persistent attempt to make Christianity credible in a scientific age."[15] We would prefer to say: "to make Christianity credible in every age."

The present generation is being raised to believe that it lives in an utterly new world—the "space-age"—a world whose novelty has no precedent in the previous intellectual pilgrimage of mankind. We are told, until we weary with its reiteration, that the world of our day differs more from that of our parents than theirs did from that of the Greeks. One may be permitted the judgment that this contrast, breath-taking as it seems, is as nothing to the readjustments of thought which were demanded of our parents and grand-parents—those who stood face-to-face with the revolutionary "new world" opened by the scientific and historical inquiries of the nineteenth century.

In any event, here is Liberal Theology's central intellectual motive: to make Christian Faith *intelligible* and *credible,* comprehensible *and* convincing to intelligent, informed and honest minds of each successive era.

To us, in our day, all this may sound obvious, platitudinous. Who would challenge it? Our inclination may be to protest, perhaps a trifle impatiently, "That's interesting, somewhat amusing history. But it has no direct relevance for us. Loyalty to truth at all costs; we take that for granted. That's a platitude."

But is it really a platitude—for us? To this query, we shall return.[16] It needs to be heard within the context of recognition that the battle for truth is *never* fully and finally won. Especially in Re-

15. In *The Christian Century,* November 3, 1933, p. 1403.

16. See, below, pp. 71ff.

ligion. Man's inherent tendency toward "wish-thinking," his fondness for "myth," his susceptibility to superstition, his vulnerability to credulity assert themselves afresh in every generation, including our own.

Liberal Theology, we have said, seeks to make Christian Faith intelligible and credible, comprehensible and convincing, to intelligent, informed and honest minds of successive periods. In the epoch of its origin, that meant to validate Christian Faith to the mind of the late nineteenth and early twentieth centuries. That mind was dominated by two mighty intellectual forces, themselves close cousins—the *scientific movement* and the *historical movement*—each something substantially *new* in human thought, and therefore presenting Christian Faith with challenges which it never previously had been compelled to face.

b. Deference to Science and the Historical Movement

In the new and freer quest for truth, men had not been left without an authoritative teacher. Rather, the authority of dogma had been displaced by the authority of Science. "The liberal Christian believes in a thoroughgoing and confident use of the scientific method of determining what is fact. . . . For the scientific method is to him one in heart with the Christian method and spirit, the very method and spirit of Jesus Christ."[17] It is important to remind ourselves of the extent to which deference to Science and its findings has been a prevailing characteristic of liberal thought. As the "Modern Mind" progressively took shape, it became ever more apparent that Christian Theology, if it were to claim and hold the allegiance of intelligent men of the day, must come to terms with *Modern Science,* not only its *methods* of discovering and testing knowledge, but also its specific

17. W. P. Merrill, *op. cit.,* p. 16.

findings regarding the Universe and man. We have quoted Dr. Bennett: "Underlying the specific convictions of liberals there is the persistent attempt to make Christianity credible in a scientific age." Current Theology is not excused from that same obligation, as we shall have occasion to note again.[18]

However, the *historical movement*—likewise in its dual aspects of a *method* of discovering the truth about the past and as a body of *conclusions*—was, in many ways, the more serious disturber. Science might challenge religious dogma from without. But historical criticism advanced directly into the domain of Christian Faith, with consequences no less drastic, challenges no less radical. And at three points. One exposes the development of Christian theology across the centuries. The second unmasks the classic formulations of Christian Faith. The third penetrates the source-spring of that Faith, the Bible.

According to unimpeachable orthodoxy, the heart of Christian Truth—all which is unchallengeable, some would say all that is essential—issued from the mind of Jesus himself, like a clear, clean, pure stream, although itself fed from many undersurface currents from his own heritage in Hebraism. As that stream flowed down the Christian centuries, it has inevitably been enlarged and enriched through currents flowing into it from extra-Christian sources. But it has also been adulterated and distorted. Distortion and adulteration have resulted partly from the opaqueness of the recipients and transmitters, due in turn to both their finitude and their perversity, partly from ingression of alien influences from other streams from foreign sources. Would anyone challenge the truth of that statement? If it is true, it carries the most radical implications for our estimate of historic Christian tradition. The test to distinguish legitimate enrichment from falsification is—congruity with the mind of Christ; nothing which contradicts the central assumptions and certitudes of that mind

18. See, below, pp. 58ff.

can be authentic Christian Truth. Without that norm, the Faith is vulnerable to the perversions which threaten religious belief always.

To change the metaphor, historic Christian Faith may be likened to an ancient ship (one of the Church's earliest and favorite figures for itself) which, in its age-long passage through the seas of thought and storms of controversy down the centuries, is forever accumulating barnacles without and refuse within. From time to time, it requires dry-docking for caustic and costly external scraping of excrescences and internal purging of dry-rot. Such cleansing is not without its perils that, in the process of purification and restoration, valid and valuable enrichments added across the ages may be excised and lost. Nevertheless, such cleansing must periodically be undertaken. Precisely that, an authentic Liberal Theology should attempt. Precisely that, the Liberal Theology of the late nineteenth and early twentieth centuries, through historical criticism, accomplished. But it is a painful, humbling, though salutary catharsis, needing to be undergone afresh in every generation.

More particularly, it is a truism of the history of Christian thought that, as one writer has put it: "Classical Christian theology is the child of the marriage between Hebrew religion and Greek philosophy. Western Catholicism was largely shaped, in its intellectual formulations, by men trained in Greek philosophy, either in the Platonism of early scholars such as Augustine, or the Aristotelianism of later scholars such as Aquinas. Palestinian Christianity increasingly assumed Greek dress." [19]

But authentic Christian Faith cannot acknowledge *that* dual parentage. Original, quintessential Christianity was born from the loins of Hebraism; from the point-of-view of Judaism, Christianity is a Jewish heresy. Jesus himself was profoundly rooted in the Hebrew

19. James Welch, *Religious Studies in an African University,* Ibadan University Press, Ibadan, Nigeria, 1950, pp. 16–17.

Scriptures of the Old Testament; he knew no other schooling, save God's teaching in and through the experiences of his own life. His conviction of God, of the world, of man, of man's destiny was that of the greatest of the prophets and psalmists, reminted, purified, enriched by his personal apprehension of God. Even Paul delighted to identify himself as "a Hebrew of the Hebrews."[20] The *substance,* the "stuff," of authentic Christian Faith is in direct continuity with the highest faith of the Old Testament.

When that Faith moved out into the Graeco-Roman world, however, it confronted precisely the challenge and the task which necessitated Liberal Theology nineteen centuries later—to make that Faith intelligible and credible to the educated minds of that day. In a profound sense, Classic Christian Theology was the earliest Liberal Theology. Those minds had been formed and moulded, before their first contacts with Christianity, by that day's dominating thought-world—*Hellenism,* deriving its presuppositions and its categories of interpretation from late Greek Philosophy. It has not been sufficiently noted that, after Paul, almost every one of the greatest and most formative Christian theologians from Ignatius of Antioch to Augustine (with the exception of Origen) was a mature thinker, deeply schooled in the Hellenistic world-view and Hellenistic ways of thinking, before he became a Christian. The result was inescapable; both the task which confronted them and their natural ways of thinking made it inevitable that they should declare their new Faith in the language of their own and their hearers' thought-world, Hellenism. *But*—here is the crucial point—the intellectual presuppositions of Hellenistic thought were, in many respects, intrinsically incompatible with, often contradictory to, Hebraic-Christian Faith; for example, the conception of God as Ineffable Substance or Intelligence rather than as Righteous Will. By the same token, the vocabulary, the language of Hellenism, was

20. Philippians 3:5.

inherently incapable of declaring authentic Christian Truth; for example, how deity and humanity could be joined in a true Person, not a monstrosity.[21]

This contrast came to decisive expression in the Christian theologians' attempt to explain the central reality of their Faith—Jesus Christ. Hence largely arose the problems, the insoluble dilemmas, *and* the unsatisfactory formulations of classic Christology. The outcome was anticipated in the Niceno-Constantinopolitan Creed (often mis-named "The Nicene Creed") with its revered phrases which are so mystifying, not to say unintelligible, to most of those who recite it: "One Lord Jesus Christ . . . Begotten of his Father before all worlds, God of God, Light of Light, Very God of Very God; Begotten, not made; Being of one substance with the Father."[22]

Four centuries of tortured and agonizing effort reached its climax in the Creed of Chalcedon. To the logical mind, it sounds like distilled nonsense. There the phrases stand, side by side, in all their seeming contradiction and glorious incredibility: "perfect in deity and perfect in humanity"—"God truly and man truly"—"begotten before the Ages of the Father . . . in the last days born of Mary the Virgin" and especially, "acknowledged in two natures, without confusion, without change, without division, without separation. . . . not

21. Much the same point has recently been put by an American Roman Catholic scholar, Professor Frank Sullivan of Loyola University: "Though the furniture of our civilization is Greek, the life of the Judeo-Christian is lived in a house built in Israel." Quoted in the *New York Times* Book Review section, November 25, 1962.

22. My memory will not surrender the recollection of a lad of twelve, struggling to memorize these phrases for his Sunday School lesson, protesting, "I don't see why I have to learn those words; I have no idea what they mean." His father, a professor of Systematic Theology, was hard put to it to make reply. How many of those who repeat these phrases, almost mechanically, week by week, really know "what they mean"? How many of their clerical mentors can make these words "intelligible and credible, comprehensible and convincing" to men and women of today?

divided or separated into two persons but one and the same Son and only begotten God Logos, Lord Jesus Christ." It is as though the Fathers were determined to affirm their certainties at whatever humiliation to reason. Their creed mirrors with fair accuracy what the Church wanted to say, but in terms which could not successfully embody its faith. No less an authority than the late William Temple summarized the outcome thus:

> "The formula of Chalcedon is, in fact, a confession of the bankruptcy of Greek Patristic Theology. The Fathers had done the best that could be done with the intellectual apparatus at their disposal. Their formula had the right devotional value; it excluded what was known to be fatal to the faith; but it explained nothing. . . . The formula merely stated the fact which constituted the problem; it did not attempt solution. It was therefore unscientific; and as theology is the science of religion, it represented the breakdown of theology." [23]

It remained for the Sixth Council of Constantinople in 680 to carry the development to its *reductio ad absurdum* in the unblushing affirmation that Christ had two wills and two energies fully operative. This is still the definitive statement of orthodox Christology. Here, indeed, is "nonsense to the philosophers" even if it be "the power of God to those who are called." The upshot of six centuries of uninterrupted labor toward an adequate interpretation of the significance of Jesus Christ is well summarized by Reinhold Seeberg: "What this Christology handed over to the Church was not a finished result but a problem—that God Himself should have lived and walked here, a man like me." [24] That was precisely the problem with which the theologians started.

"Bankruptcy," "breakdown"—these are harsh and devastating verdicts to pronounce upon classical Christian creedal formulation. They

23. In *Foundations,* ed. by B. H. Streeter, Macmillan, 1913, pp. 230–31.

24. *Lehrbuch d. Dogmengeschichte,* A. Deichert, 1895, I. 231.

are declared by a responsible theologian of highest competence and unmatched eminence. They do not exaggerate the quagmires and distortions of tradition from which Liberal Theology offered deliverance and corrective.

Nevertheless, the historical movement of the late nineteenth century was not wholly caustic in its effect upon Christian Faith, however necessary and salutary that cleansing may have been. It brought one positive contribution to Christian interpretation so valuable that its worth more than outweighs the negative conclusions. Historical inquiry uncovered and set forth a fresh, clear and compelling portrait of Christian Faith's originating and authoritative source, Jesus of Nazareth—rescued, it was sometimes said, from the "graveclothes" of tradition, perhaps better from the straitjacket of tradition—linking Modern Thought with vital Evangelical Faith and supplying something of a bond between what we have ventured to call Liberal Theology's "male" and its "female" parents. Thus it made available the *content* for Liberal Theology's first and major debt to its other parent, Evangelicalism—Jesus Christ, the fulcrum of Christian Faith; and it made possible Liberal Theology's controlling positive conviction—the centrality of Jesus Christ. To this we shall return below.

c. Tentativeness as to Metaphysical Certainty

It has not always been sufficiently noted how profoundly the outlook to which Liberal Theology was heir was penetrated by an enervating metaphysical scepticism, and how far the child had inherited the parental paralysis. Partly, this was a reflection of the avowed tentativeness of Science. More largely, however, it was a direct heritage from the influence of Immanuel Kant, with his absolute dichotomy between the realm of phenomena or "things-as-they-appear" of which men may gain a kind of practical control through Science, and the realm of genuine or ultimate reality, "things-as-they-really-are" to which access for the human mind is completely and forever barred.[25] In Ritschl, this dualism became the distinction between the truths of fact which are the province of Science and philosophy, and judgments of value which are the distinctive province of theology.[26] Through Ritschl, this dualistic view of human knowledge worked its way into the liberal Christian mind where, finding ready alliance with one of the most marked features of the evangelical spirit, the emphasis upon Christian experience, it encouraged indifference to natural theology, disdain of metaphysics, and reliance upon the evidence of religious experience as our sole and all-sufficient guide to the truth about God.[27] To minds of a later generation schooled in a sterner realism which could not so dichotomize God's world, it seemed to propose a "double standard of truth," to subject truth to purely pragmatic testing, and to induce a withering scepticism in men's certainty of God.

d. The Assumption of Continuity

Modern Thought not only inducted Liberal Theology into scientific and historical methods, with their stringent purging of superstition and distortion in the Christian Tradition. It also supplied Liberal Theology with its *basic theoretical assumption,* what Dr. John C. Bennett has rightly identified as the presupposition of all Liberal Theology:

> "Running through liberalism's whole theology there has been the assumption of continuity in the world—continuity between revela-

25. Cf. below, pp. 163ff.

26. Ritschl followed Lotze rather than Kant in his theory of knowledge, but Kant's agnosticism infected his attitude, and even more that of many of his followers.

27. Cf. below, pp. 38ff.

> tion and natural religion, between Christianity and other religions, between the saved and the lost, between Christ and other men, between man and God."[28]

Dr. Bennett's dictum is confirmed in the latest comprehensive review and critique of Liberal Theology. Searching for "Formative Factors in American Liberalism," Professor Kenneth Cauthen discovers, as the first of the "Underlying Principles of Liberalism": "Continuity."[29]

The principle of continuity received great impetus from the concept of *Evolution*. It found theological expression in the idea of immanence which has been called the "most characteristic theological doctrine of the nineteenth century."[30] It tended to melt the traditional antithesis of natural and supernatural into a vague *monism*. It furnished ground for men's confidence in *progress*. It bred a new and more sympathetic *tolerance toward other religions, and toward no religion*. It encouraged men to look into *their own highest experience* for clearest light on the divine nature. It opened the way for a new interpretation of Christ's divinity through his humanity, thus restoring the *Incarnation* to a central importance. Above all, it fostered a *lofty estimate of man and his potentialities for achievement,* both spiritual and material, and confident expectancy of the realization of a Christian society in the not too distant future. Indeed, the genius of Liberal optimism may be identified with its confidence in man's God-given capacities to discern truth, in his responsiveness to the highest, in the

28. J. C. Bennett, *op. cit.,* p. 1403.

29. *The Impact of American Religious Liberalism,* p. 6.

30. See A. C. McGiffert's article, "Immanence," in Hastings, *Encyclopaedia of Religion and Ethics,* Vol. VII, pp. 167ff. Cf. also Chaps. IX and X in his *The Rise of Modern Religious Ideas.* "Both evolution and immanence represent the same general tendency to emphasize unity, which is a marked characteristic of modern times. In the one case it is unity of process, binding all existence together; in the other it is unity of force or substance, making all things the expression of one all-pervading divine energy or of one all-embracing divine being." (p. 201)

possibility of attaining a loftier fulfillment of personal life and the social order. These were all characteristic features of the prevailing secular outlook, absorbed within the marrow of Liberal Theology.

This inventory of the indebtedness of Liberal Theology to the Modern Mind would not be complete, however, without reiterated emphasis upon the attitude of dispassionate tolerance, of open-minded receptivity, of confidence in "sweet reasonableness" as well as in the powers of human reason, of modesty in personal profession, of preference for understatement rather than over-statement, of respect for human personality, of loyalty to justice, honor and truth, which characterizes true liberalism everywhere and always, and is one of its most precious gifts to the life of religion.

2. RELIGIOUS EVANGELICALISM

To identify Liberal Theology in terms of its relation to trends of thought dominant in the Modern Period, whether of the eighteen-eighties or of the nineteen-sixties, is to tell just half the story, and perhaps the less important half—like explaining a person in terms of his or her inheritance from one parent. Any account badly misses the mark which does not place equal stress upon another development, not basically theological at all, which paralleled trends of thought and furnished spiritual undergirding and dynamic for them. At its birth, Liberal Theology sprang from a rediscovery, a renewal, of vital and dynamic experience of God—the living God made known in, by and through Jesus Christ. If the disintegration of confidence in traditional dogma which characterized the closing decades of the nineteenth century and the opening decades of the twentieth had not been paralleled by a widespread renewal of personal religion, the history of Christian thought in that period would have been very different from what it is.

Dr. Henry Sloane Coffin was never wearied in insisting that the only proper identification of Liberal Theology is "Liberal Evangelicalism":

> "Liberal evangelicalism! Note which word in our title stands merely in the qualifying position of the adjective and which occupies the position of eminence as the noun. We are first and foremost evangelicals—evangelicals to the core of our spiritual beings. . . . And we are liberals—not liberals in the sense that we cultivate freedom for its own sake, but for the gospel's sake. We are liberals on behalf of our evangelicalism."

No one who has not known, either personally in his own life or vicariously through parents or grandparents, the reality and power of Evangelical Christian Faith can really comprehend the inner character of Liberal Theology. Sad to say, that is equipment largely lacking in the present generation.

From its second parent, Liberal Theology also drew a rich inheritance which, likewise, was fourfold:

a. The Authority of Christian Experience

When Christians could no longer rest upon familiar orthodoxy for the certainty which living faith requires, the more scholarly might look to the new teacher, Science. For the great mass of ordinary folk, this was quite impracticable. Happily there was available to them the needed assurance in a far more accessible and far surer source—in the witness of their own personal religious life. The Romantic Movement had prepared the way by centering attention upon inner experiences. The spirit of the time was subjective, individualistic, mystical. For Christians, the crumbling of external bulwarks—Scripture, Church and dogma—deepened the mood of uncertainty, of introspection. And now there swept through their ranks a vivid and all-compelling discovery of the presence of God, "the living Christ," within their own spirits. Why trouble about formal and external validation when so intimate and so undeniable a certainty ruled their very souls? As Tennyson wrote:

> "Speak to Him, thou, for He hears, and Spirit with Spirit can meet—
> Closer is He than breathing, and nearer than hands and feet." [31]

In this nearer and surer pathway, liberal theologians followed. This was clearly foreshadowed by Dr. Lewis F. Stearns of Bangor Seminary when he was asked to interpret the American situation before the International Congregational Council in London in 1891. He said, in part:

> "Let us look now at some of our present tendencies. We mark, first, a movement toward a more spiritual conception of Christianity. . . . We have been too prone to regard Christianity as a system of abstract truths and of remote historical facts. Notions and propositions have been more to us than the great spiritual realities for which they stand, the sacred events of nineteen hundred years ago more than the redemptive facts of today. . . . We are coming to understand that it is the recognition of the invincible reality of spiritual Christianity which is going to give our theology its great power in the future . . . Criticism may assail the historical facts of revelation; rationalism may urge objections to its doctrines; but the surf on our coast of Maine might as easily overthrow the granite cliffs against which it breaks as criticism and rationalism disturb the Christian realities which stand firm in the experience of the individual believer and the church." [32]

31. Alfred Tennyson, "The Higher Pantheism."

32. L. F. Stearns, "The Present Direction of Theological Thought in the Congregational Churches of the United States," in *Present Day Theology,* Scribners, 1893, pp. 533ff.

A similar emphasis upon Christian experience was reiterated in every characteristic confession of the liberal position. In 1898, on the occasion of his inauguration as Professor of Systematic Theology at Union Seminary, Dr. William Adams Brown said:

> "What is this work to which you call me? . . . Are the doctrines which form the subject matter of our science dogmas to be received on authority, irrespective of their contents; or are they living convictions, born of experience, and maintaining themselves in spite of all opposition because of the response which they wake in the hearts and consciences of men? . . .
>
> "It is this connection with experience which gives to the work of the theologian at once its dignity and its interest." [33]

In the same year there came from the pen of William Newton Clarke the first attempt at a comprehensive and systematic exposition of the "new theology" which opened with these sentences:

> "Theology is preceded by religion as botany by the life of plants. Religion is the reality of which theology is the study . . . Theology thus deals only with the realities which make up religion, and with them only as they enter religion." [34]

The position was most fully worked out by Ritschl with his determination to rest the whole weight of Christian faith upon the experience of reconciliation through Christ.[35] Ritschl was the most influential theologian of the late nineteenth century, and the principal teacher of American liberals.

33. W. A. Brown, *Christ the Vitalizing Principle of Christian Theology,* W. C. Martin, 1898, pp. 19–20.

34. *An Outline of Christian Theology,* Scribners, 1898, pp. 1, 2.

35. *Justification and Reconciliation,* espec. Vol. III. The emphasis upon religious experience roots back in Ritschl's great predecessor, Friedrich Schleiermacher. See his *Discourses on Religion* (1799), *Soliloquies* (1800), and *The Christian Faith* (1822). Cf. pp. 176ff., below.

b. The Centrality of Jesus Christ

At the heart of Evangelical Liberalism stands Jesus Christ. With some, this central place is taken by the man, Jesus of Nazareth, "the Historical Jesus" or *"the Jesus of History,"* reclaimed by the historical studies of recent years, and now gladly affirmed as both the source and the norm of true Christian Faith. For others, it has been *"the Living Christ,"* an intimate Presence within one's own soul (an almost unknown reality for the present generation, one suspects, a phrase without meaning, certainly lacking "existential" reality). But, for normative Evangelical Liberals, *the Jesus of History* and *the Living Christ* are a single organic, indissoluble personal reality. That reality is defined in the life, words, deeds, mind, spirit, faith of *Jesus of Nazareth;* it is known in present power in the *Living Christ.*[36]

The main point is: Liberal Theology in every one of its authentic expressions has been *through and through Christocentric.* More than that; it has been the most determinedly Christocentric theology in Christian history. Indeed, the contention may be advanced that Evangelical Liberalism is the *first* thoroughly and consistently Christocentric theology *in the authentic meaning of that term,* i.e. understanding of God, of man, of human destiny; taking with utter seriousness the central Christian conviction—that God was definitively present in Jesus of Nazareth.

That this was, and is, the distinctive mark and the decisive characteristic of Liberal Theology, there would appear no ground for question. Adolph Harnack, the most influential "Liberal" German theologian, speaking to the question: "What is the Christian religion?", replied: "The answer seems to be simple and at the same time exhaustive: Jesus Christ and his Gospel."[37] We have already cited

36. Cf. further below, pp. 108ff.

37. *What is Christianity?*, Putnam, 1901, p. 10.

Dr. Lewis F. Stearns' remarkable report of theological trends in the United States in the early 1890s. Following his exposition of the new emphasis upon the witness of Christian Experience, Dr. Stearns goes on to declare:

> "We are coming more distinctly to recognize the central place of the living Christ in our theological thought. . . . We are less disposed than of old to speculate upon these high subjects, more willing to admit the mystery. It is the Christ himself, in all his living, saving power, upon whom our thought is concentrated, whom we strive to hold up to men, and in whom we find the key to all the problems of religious thought.
>
> "The way is thus being opened for a larger and richer conception of God. We are trying to 'Christologize' our doctrine of God, to set Him forth as He is seen in the face of Jesus Christ. It is often said that we are coming to a more ethical conception of God. It is more ethical because it is more Christian, because it is not of the God of Nature, but of the God and Father of our Lord Jesus Christ." [38]

Dr. William Adams Brown, one of the earliest and best balanced American Liberal theologians, took as the theme of his inaugural address: "Christ the Vitalizing Principle of Christian Theology," and declared: "The new school raises the old cry, 'Back to Christ.' Let no theology call itself Christian which has not its center and source in Him." [39] Dr. William Pierson Merrill likewise voiced the central affirmation of those early Liberals: "Whatever else may be doubtful about the religion and theology of the liberal Christian, this is sure, that it loses and finds itself wholly in Christ. . . . The liberal would move, live and have his whole being in Christ." [40] And Robert Browning, poet supreme of Liberal Christians, cried:

38. Stearns, *op. cit.*

39. Brown, *op. cit.*, p. 23.

40. *Liberal Christianity*, p. 48.

"I say, the acknowledgment of God in Christ
Accepted by thy reason, solves for thee
All questions in the earth and out of it."[41]

On this point, later and more critical Liberals have been no less emphatic. Thus, Dr. John C. Bennett in "After Liberalism—What?":

"A [third] contribution of liberalism is its emphasis upon the Jesus of History. . . . The liberal emphasis on the historical Jesus has provided the norm for the criticism and simplification of the Christian tradition. . . . It is only in the human life of Jesus, in his personality and his teaching, that the word is revealed to men in its fulness. . . . We can grant all that may be said about the cosmic significance of Christ or about the contemporary Christ, but what we learn about the cosmos from Christ comes centrally from the Jesus of history and what we recognize as the contemporary Christ we must judge by its congruence with the Jesus of history as the norm."[42]

So, also, the two most recent contemporary critiques, both still damp from the presses, one by the young Christian theologian already quoted who writes from a chair of Theology in a Protestant seminary, the other by a precocious young philosopher who has moved beyond conventional Christian allegiance, agree in assuming the same basic truth regarding Liberal Theology:

". . . The historical Jesus became the focal point of liberal Christology."

"Liberalism took another step in the right direction in regarding the humanity of Jesus seriously . . . A subtle docetism has always haunted the theology of the past, even when its more obvious forms were denounced. Liberal thinkers overcame this hesitancy to regard Jesus as fully man and called the attention of the church to the truth that whatever else he was, he was a human being in

41. *A Death in the Desert.*

42. *Op. cit.*, pp. 1403–04.

the fullest sense of the word. . . . Liberalism made a substantial contribution to theology by putting an end to docetism."[43]

"For most liberal Protestants, the historical Jesus was their strong ally in the battle against Calvinist orthodoxy and social injustice. Jesus was the great general of the Liberal Protestants in the fight for a regeneration of culture."[44]

That this *is* the central Christian conviction—"God was in Christ"—no responsible student of Christianity is likely to challenge. No single text is more often uttered as embodying the heart, the essence, of Christian Faith than Paul's declaration to the Christians in Corinth: "God was in Christ reconciling the world to himself."[45] This is the affirmation of "the Incarnation"; and the Incarnation is the fulcrum, the pivot, the regnant certainty of Christianity.

This certainty has always been difficult if not impossible to believe, even more difficult clearly and convincingly to explain and justify. This was the "scandal" of Christian affirmation from the outset—"a stumbling-block to Jews" (i.e. the traditionally devout), "folly, utter nonsense to Greeks" (i.e. the sophisticated).[46]

The fact is—and this is one of the most important and neglected facts of Christian history—Christians themselves, perhaps especially Christian theologians, have seldom been able to accept the central conviction of their Faith at face value. Deviation, departure from that determinative conviction has, from the outset and even today, been in

43. Kenneth Cauthen, *The Impact of American Religious Liberalism,* Harper & Row, 1962, pp. 25, 219–20. The recognition that historic Christology has been "haunted by docetism" echoes Dr. D. M. Baillie's dictum, quoted below, p. 45.

44. William Warren Bartley III, *The Retreat to Commitment,* Knopf, 1962, pp. 31, 32.

45. II Corinthians 5:19 (It is noteworthy that the rendering into English in most of the standard translations is virtually identical).

46. I Corinthians 1:23.

either of two opposite directions—either the assertion that Jesus was truly a man but no more than a man, not really God-in-human-flesh, i.e. Ebionism in the Early Church, Humanism or Unitarianism in our day, *or* the affirmation that Jesus was God but not really a man, i.e. Docetism or Semi-docetism. However, the latter deviation—affirmation of the deity of Christ but explicit or implicit qualification of his true and full humanity—has been much the more persistent heresy. The truth is: Christian Theology's account of its central reality—Jesus Christ—has always been somewhat heretical. This is the judgment of one whose interpretation of the history has won well-nigh universal acclaim from virtually all schools of contemporary Christian Theology, Professor D. M. Baillie:

> "The Church . . . . was continually haunted by a docetism [denial of the true and full humanity of Jesus] which made His human nature very different from ours and indeed largely explained it away as a matter of simulation or 'seeming' rather than reality". . . . "The cruder forms of docetism were fairly soon left behind, but in its more subtle forms the danger continued in varying degrees to dog the steps of theology right through the ages until modern times." [47]

In summary: Christian Faith's explanation of its central conviction has been semi-docetic, i.e. always somewhat and sometimes greatly heretical—*"until modern times."*

If Liberal Theology holds validity, it is precisely because its interpretation of Jesus Christ is most fully adequate, most true to authentic Christian Faith. By the same token, Liberal Theology's enduring significance rests upon the decision whether it offers just another among the Christologies of the Christian centuries *or* whether in fact it declares the most genuinely "orthodox" Christology in Christian history,

47. D. M. Baillie, *God Was in Christ,* Scribners, 1948, pp. 11, 20.

and whether that understanding and interpretation of Jesus Christ can be "credible and convincing" to intelligent, informed, honest minds of today.

If this claim for Liberal Theology is correct—that, more than any predecessor or alternative rendering of Christian Faith, it is based squarely upon Jesus Christ and takes with utmost seriousness, as its determinative and regulative norm, the Faith of Jesus of Nazareth, then it must be recognized as something genuinely *new* in Christian thought. Then, it stands, *not* as just another in the two millennia of Christian Theologies, but rather a return to and reclamation of the one authentic center of Christian Faith, from which all Christian Theology must proceed and by which it must be judged. That does not imply that Evangelical Liberalism is the final Christian Theology. It does imply that here is a decisive water-shed in the history of Christian Theology. As Professor D. M. Baillie affirmed—and his affirmation appears to have gone virtually unchallenged: "We can never go back to the pre-Jesus of History Christology." To say the same thing positively: Christian Theology must go forward from, and upon the basis of, Liberal Theology.

c. Loyalty to the Historic Faith

In striking contrast to other theological expressions of the Liberal Movement which did not maintain their center of reference inside the Church, Evangelical Liberalism was determined to continue fully within the main stream of historic Christian development. At first, this was accomplished by use of the principle of growth so congenial to the thought of the time; the "new theology" is the "fuller flowering" of what had been implicit in traditional beliefs. So, Dr. Stearns:

> "The substance of our theology is to be found now, as always, in the great unchanging facts and truths of Christianity accepted in every

> age of the church. . . . So, if we speak of a 'new theology,' we mean that it is new only as a living body is new at each fresh stage of its growth, conserving and fulfilling the one type that runs through all its changes, and that is neither old or new." [48]

Later, recourse was had to the principle of "reinterpretation"; modern theology is mainly translation of the truths of the ancient faith into language familiar and understandable to the modern age. Finally, Liberal Theology came more and more to rely upon a distinction given wide currency through the influence of Dr. Fosdick—the recognition of "abiding experiences in changing categories." [49] Not only does the language of theology change. So also do concepts which that language seeks to express. But the "experiences" which lie behind the concepts are the same from one generation to another. Thus, identity with the historic faith was established through the "principle of continuity"; and the locus of continuity was discovered at the heart of personal "Christian experience."

d. Moral and Social Compassion and Dedication

Evangelicalism began, as we have seen, in a rediscovery of the *centrality of Jesus Christ.* It bore its most notable fruit in profound *moral concern and social compassion,* and in unwearying *dedication* to the fulfillment of their directives. The latter was a direct result of the former.

Evangelicalism was in no sense mainly a theological development. Rather, it was a resurgence of vibrant and dynamic spiritual vitality. Its genius was for propagation rather than for formulation. It lifted men's vision to the horizons of their world. And it deepened their insight into the realities of that world's corporate life. It quickened

48. *Op. cit.*

49. See, especially, H. E. Fosdick, *The Modern Use of the Bible,* Macmillan, 1924, Chap. IV.

consciences to needs and injustices and opportunities and obligations which had largely escaped the attention and eluded the concern of the antecedent orthodoxy. It also filled them with an assurance of what the spirit of Christ might, through them, accomplish for the purification and uplifting of mankind's life. And it steeled them for unmeasured devotion that that hope might be translated into fact—an assurance and a hope which we now know to have been overconfident, some would say naïve. Nevertheless, it was fecund, germinative, prolific to an extent unparalleled in any other period of Christian history. In the short space of less than a century, there came forth from it the most remarkable series of movements for the improvement of human life and the spread of Christian Faith across the world in the nineteen centuries of our era. Heightened missionary conviction and dedication which carried Christianity to the ends of the earth and have planted the Christian Church in virtually every land; conviction of the responsibility of Christians to transform the structures of society as well as the lives of individuals; compassion for the underprivileged in great cities, in industrial communities and in rural and neglected areas; new concern for "Christian nurture" of the young; lastly, conviction of sin for the "scandal of Christian divisions" and resolve to effect unity among Christians and their Churches—all these were the fruit of Evangelicalism; in all of them, Liberal Theology was a participant and, in no small measure, the inspiring power.[50]

50. Cf. the author's *For the Healing of the Nations: Impressions of Christianity Around the World; What IS the Church Doing?; They Found the Church There: The Armed Forces Discover Christian Missions; World Christianity: Yesterday, Today, and Tomorrow; One Great Ground of Hope: Christian Missions and Christian Unity.*

CHAPTER THREE

THE INDICTMENT OF LIBERAL THEOLOGY

1. SERVITUDE TO MODERN CULTURE

a. Uncritical Deference to Science

b. Optimism Regarding Man and Social Progress

c. Moralism

2. DISCONTINUITY VS. CONTINUITY

CHAPTER THREE

THE INDICTMENT OF LIBERAL THEOLOGY

For two decades and more, Liberal Theology has been widely in disrepute. It was in 1933, as was noted in the Preface, that Dr. John Bennett, himself a dutiful son of the liberal tradition who probably would not wish to disavow his patrimony, identified its plight as "disintegration" and added: "Disintegration may seem too strong a word, but I am using it quite literally." [1] In the same year, 1933, I myself had reiterated and developed somewhat further the diagnosis presented two years earlier as "The Sickness of Liberal Religion": [2]

> "There is no more significant feature of the contemporary religious mood than the increasing disillusion with liberal theology. Wherever thoughtful Christians gather, there are references to the sickness of liberal religion, to its failure to stem the ebbing tide of religious loyalty among educated people, to its patent inadequacy for a moment like the present. One detects mounting agreement that Liberalism has served its mission but is now outmoded." [3]

1. *The Christian Century,* November 3, 1933, p. 1403.
2. In *The World Tomorrow,* August 1931.
3. *The Plain Man Seeks for God,* Scribners, 1933, pp. 24–26.

"Disillusion" with Liberal Theology, the recognition of the "disintegration" of Liberalism are, therefore, in no sense contemporary phenomena; they have been an accepted common-place of theological thought and discussion for over a quarter-century. As I have suggested in the Preface to this volume, the intervening decades have witnessed no marked change in the theological atmosphere, no alleviation of the discredit of Liberal Theology. The "existential situation" to which these pages are addressed is very similar to that obtaining when these somber diagnoses were offered. For many, Liberal Theology's perspective is discredited, its conclusions disproven, its pretensions disdained. Some have proclaimed its demise, although that announcement, like Mark Twain's famous obituary, may be said to be "somewhat exaggerated."

In any event, clearly the time is ripe for a thoroughgoing critical reappraisal. By interesting coincidence, probably the two most notable critiques of Liberal Theology yet forthcoming have appeared, as we have observed above, within recent months, both from outside—one from the left, from a stance beyond the limits of conventional Christian allegiance; the other from the right, from a position which professes adherence to Christian orthodoxy—both by able young scholars, one of whom began his intellectual pilgrimage within the orbit of Liberal Theology,[4] the other of whom confesses that he "grew up being told that liberalism was a bad word" and that his theological outlook "has been shaped by the dominant developments in post-liberal (*sic*) theology."[5] The first has moved "beyond liberalism" to develop an original agnostic rationalism; the other appears to be moving from an avowal of neo-orthodoxy toward a conviction which builds directly upon Liberal Theology. A member of an older generation who is not

4. William Warren Bartley III, *The Retreat to Commitment,* Knopf, 1962.

5. Kenneth Cauthen, *The Impact of American Religious Liberalism,* Harper and Row, 1962, pp. xi, 213.

ashamed to declare himself, like Professor Robert L. Calhoun, "a liberal bandaged but unbowed," may be permitted to undertake a reappraisal of Liberal Theology "from within," from a chastened but convinced adherence.

Any responsible reappraisal should be made in two contexts—retrospective and prospective—on the one hand, re-examining, assessing and, where necessary, correcting widely prevalent conceptions, and misconceptions, of how Liberal Theology arose, what influences determined its character, what in essence it actually was; on the other hand, scrutinizing and judging its contemporary validity and value as an authentic, adequate and persuasive interpretation of Christian Faith for "informed, intelligent and honest minds" of today and tomorrow.[6]

A *retrospective* examination of the origins and character of Liberal Theology has been attempted in the previous section of this book under the caption, "The Ancestry of Liberal Theology," and, more fully, in the appended essay on "The Farther Background: Theology in the Nineteenth Century." One or two brief comments may be added before we turn from an historical perspective toward critical assessment of Liberal Theology's validity and adequacy to guide Christian thinking in the days ahead.

For example, it is impressive, and important, to note that the initial reaction from Liberalism, the most damning early indictments, originated not from without, whether from the left or from the right, but from within. Moreover, while Continental European theologians—Karl Barth and Emil Brunner in the early phase, latterly Rudolf Bultmann and his disciples—have made their impact upon American thought, it has been an American theologian of massive competence and towering eminence whose condemnation has been most trenchant

6. This is the sequence of discussion in the two recently published critiques of Liberal Theology just cited.

and influential—my distinguished colleague and beloved friend, Reinhold Niebuhr. In an autobiographical *confessio* of the development of his thinking through the decade of the nineteen-thirties, captioned "Ten Years That Shook My World," [7] Dr. Niebuhr avowed the "rejection of almost all the liberal theological ideals and ideas with which I ventured forth [upon his ministry] in 1915." This disavowal could be documented in detail from the whole, large corpus of Dr. Niebuhr's early writings. It is echoed in the voices of his disciples of the 1930s, 40s, and 50s. It should be noted further, however, that the rebellious children of Liberal Theology, while indicting and disavowing their parentage, continue to carry, far more than they are prepared to acknowledge, the imprint of their lineage. It is highly significant that the closing sentences of the contemporary volume which has subjected Liberal Theology to its most thoroughgoing critique and rejection in favor of an avowed neo-orthodoxy, should declare: "Neo-orthodoxy is a continuation of liberalism in that in both method and content it is dependent upon liberal insights. The leading contemporary thinkers began their careers under liberal influences and have retained the distinct impress of their family background even as they have criticized their theological fathers." [8] And Dr. Reinhold Niebuhr, author of the most devastating early disavowal of Liberal Theology, wrote in 1960: "When I find Neo-orthodoxy turning into sterile orthodoxy or a new Scholasticism, I find that I am a liberal at heart, and that many of my broadsides at Liberalism were indiscriminate." [9]

This characteristically frank and humble recantation by Liberal Theology's severest critic provides the ideal stance from which to

7. *The Christian Century,* April 26, 1939, p. 542.

8. Cauthen, *op. cit.,* p. 255.

9. *The Christian Century,* May 11, 1960, p. 568.

reassess its validity and importance for tomorrow. This can best be done, in the first instance, by examining the charges against it.

I. SERVITUDE TO MODERN CULTURE

What, then is the major indictment levelled against Liberal Theology? The well-nigh unanimous reply of Liberal Theology's critics is: *Servitude to Modern Culture*. Dr. Cauthen is not mistaken in interpreting the conflict of Liberal Theology and its alternatives in terms of the confrontation of Christian Faith and Modern Thought—precisely the issue on which, as we noted, Liberal Theology took its rise. The overarching indictment is: in striving to make Christian Faith intelligible and convincing to the "mind" bred in modern culture, Christian theologians have fallen victims to that culture's illusions and aberrations. Thus, Reinhold Niebuhr: "The adjustment of modern religion to the 'mind' of modern culture inevitably involved capitulation to its thin 'soul'."[10] "The liberal culture of modernity is defective in both religious profundity and political sagacity . . . It understands neither the heights to which life may rise nor the depths to which it may sink. . . . It is quite unable to give guidance and direction to a confused generation which faces the disintegration of a social system and the task of building a new one."[11] In this caveat, critics from outside have been joined by Liberal Theology's own most outstanding and influential interpreter from the pulpit, Dr. Harry Emerson Fosdick, in a bold and widely quoted sermon entitled, "Beyond Modernism": "In the new enterprise the watchword will be not, Accommodate yourself to the prevailing culture! but, Stand out from it and challenge it! . . . We cannot harmonize Christ himself with

10. *An Interpretation of Christian Ethics,* Harper, 1935, p. 15.

11. Reinhold Niebuhr, *Reflections on the End of an Era,* Scribners, 1934, p. ix.

modern culture. What Christ does to modern culture is to challenge it."[12]

My diagnosis of the "sickness of liberal religion" reported the then-prevailing indictment thus: "The most serious indictment of the theology of the liberal churches during the past quarter-century is that, with sincere intentions, it has betrayed the cause of true religion. In seeking to save religious belief from annihilation by the accepted thought-forms of the secular world, it has become a pallid reflection of the secular philosophy. More and more it has been content to accept for religion the status of an incidental interest in life. Indeed no choice was left it. Contemporary thought has catalogued religion as one among life's avocational concerns. Youth's verdict is sound: 'Religion has become an elective in the university of life.' Liberalism has bowed a tacit acquiescence, and in so doing has acknowledged the ultimate demise of religion. More and more it has preached what might be termed a 'minimum interpretation of religion.' Increasingly it has tended to speak of 'religion' rather than of Christianity; of religion without explicit reference to the certainty and necessity of God, but rather as a 'way of life' or 'philosophy of life'; of Jesus as the best of men; of prayer as synonymous with worship or aspiration. In its solicitude to domesticate religion within the fabric of modern thought, religion has become hardly distinguishable from ethics, the religious life from the noblest secular life."[13]

The critics of Liberal Theology are in revolt, one may say rebellion, against Modern Culture, both its life and its thought, i.e. its ethos. More specifically, it is charged, Liberal Theology has bowed the knee and accepted uncritically and mistakenly these features of the Modern Outlook:

12. H. E. Fosdick, "Beyond Modernism" in *The Christian Century,* December 4, 1935.

13. *The Plain Man Seeks for God,* Scribners, pp. 25–26.

a. Its *deference to Science*—both methods and conclusions.

b. Its romantic *optimism regarding man's nature* and its utopian *expectations of social progress.*

c. Its *"Moralism."*

Thus, the issues are sharply drawn. What shall our judgment be?

Let it be recognized at once that the factors which have fashioned the lineaments of "Modern Thought" are not one but legion; their interplay and mutual fructification furnish a riddle for the most acute historical criticism. But within this mesh of confused influences, two (not one) are so much the most important as to warrant special classification. Indeed, most of the other important factors may be traced, directly or indirectly, to them.

On the whole, these two forces took their rise in quite different sources. They have converged to bring a single impact upon modern thinking. Indeed they have proven extraordinarily effective teammates; they have played into each other's hands like trained acrobats. The one factor was largely theoretical; it began as a temper of mind. The other was predominantly practical; it came as a temper of life. The first is the critical, sceptical *intellectual outlook* which was born of the thought of David Hume and Immanuel Kant, was furthered by the rise of a scientific philosophy, and has come more and more to dominate the serious reflection of the nineteenth and twentieth centuries. The other is the character of *modern civilization,* the actual mechanized fabric of daily living as Science has made it possible for us. The first has won a growing ascendancy over men's thinking; the other has increasingly determined men's living. The roots of our present situation are, then, mainly two—the one in the dominant thought-currents of the past century and a half, the other in the kind of life which modern man has built for himself.

The intellectual problem was given its initial if not its clearest and soundest formulation by Immanuel Kant. Indeed it is a truism that any discussion of Modern Thought, whether philosophical or theological, must make its start with him. The main outlines of his position, for good or for ill or for both, have provided the issues for the intellectual battles since his day and have set the terms within which those issues should be debated.

An examination of the thought of Immanuel Kant and his successors, of their dominating influence upon nineteenth-century theologians, and of the outworking of this influence, especially through Friedrich Schleiermacher, George Wilhelm Friedrich Hegel, Albrecht Ritschl and their disciples, upon Liberal Theology in general and American Liberalism in particular lies outside the scope of the present study.[14] Nevertheless, as we turn to confront and assess the indictment of Liberal Theology advanced by its critics, focussing so largely on its "deference to Science," we should carry firmly in mind the double recognition—that not one but two factors, closely interrelated to be sure, *both* the presuppositions and structure of "Modern Thought" *and* the actualities of "Modern Life," have played continuously upon Christian Faith in the recent period; *and* that, within the first of these factors, "Modern Thought," not one but two influences, likewise reciprocally effective, joined, *both* the philosophical development from Kant onward *and* the scientific outlook.

Within the context of that twofold recognition, let us consider the specifics of the indictment of Liberal Theology.

a. Uncritical Deference to Science

Dialogue between Science and Theology has been a continuing motif of Modern Thought. But it must always be remembered that

14. See "The Farther Background: Theology in the Nineteenth Century," below, pp. 155ff.

Science presents itself in three distinguishable although not unrelated phases—as a *method* of ascertaining truth, as specific *findings* thus discovered, and, more generally but also more pervasively, as ***an attitude and spirit;*** i.e.,

scientific method: analysis, description, classification, generalization.

scientific truth: the conception of the world and man attained by Science.

scientific spirit: loyalty to scientifically established truths and scepticism beyond that.

As a *method* of ascertaining truth, Science has registered its great triumphs in knowledge of physical nature. But, as thought moves upward from external nature through human nature to the realm of values, the realities sought to be understood are progressively less susceptible to analysis, to precise description, above all to classification and generalization. In consequence, scientific method is less and less applicable. However, it is precisely with the unique imponderables of spirit and its values that religious faith is above all concerned.

Scientific method determines *scientific truth*—such truths as yield to analysis, description, classification and generalization. In the larger quest for Truth, for knowledge of Reality, however, Science offers a real but limited usefulness.

As we shall have occasion to note, it is in its less precise but also more pervasive aspect, the *scientific spirit,* i.e. confidence in scientifically proven truths joined with scepticism regarding any "truths" which lie outside the purview and mastery of scientific method, that Modern Science has exerted perhaps its largest influence upon Modern Thought.

These generalizations require to be subjected to a more detailed and discriminating scrutiny and appraisal of the "outlook" of Modern

Science—as *method,* as *truth,* and as *spirit*—and its impact upon the point-of-view of the non-scientific layman.[15]

The early conclusions of Modern Science and the earliest notable "scientific philosophy" in the writings of Newton were among the influences to awaken Kant from his "dogmatic slumber" and set his energies to the development of his critical philosophy. And the critical, sceptical intellectual temper to which his philosophy gave birth was furthered by the later scientific philosophy until it came almost to dominate the thought of the nineteenth century. However, it is not the impact of scientific theory upon the speculation of the period which interests us most, but the far more immediate and obvious effect of scientific ways of thinking and scientific achievements upon the religious outlook of the ordinary citizen. For the same sets of forces which were so powerfully moulding theory were also making their imprint directly upon lay attitudes, though in somewhat different ways.

It is a common-place among students of the history of thought that Modern Science introduced almost no startling new difficulties for religion, no problems which had not been acutely sensed by the Greeks and made the objects of serious study through the centuries. Not the discovery of new facts but the dissemination of a new outlook created the "Modern Mind." Many years ago, Professor Höffding wrote: "It is not so much the results at which science is arriving, or has arrived, which bring about the quarrel between science and religion, and condition the religious problem; but rather the whole trend of ideas, the entire habit of mind which empirical science has fostered in those who have developed under its influence."[16] The immense influence

15. The pages which follow represent a revision, condensation and updating of the discussion of the same issues in *The Plain Man Seeks for God,* pp. 55–67 (Copyright, 1933 by Charles Scribner's Sons).

16. Quoted in John Douglas Adam, *Under the Highest Leadership,* Association Press, 1917, p. 2.

of Science in the nineteenth century was due to the fact that then, for the first time in human history, the "scientific outlook" became the possession, one might almost say the prepossession, of the common man. As Whitehead so clearly points out, every period of civilization has had thinkers characterized by that outlook—the passion for facts linked to suspicion of metaphysical speculation which mark the scientific temper of mind. But they have been solitary figures, for the most part confined to the cloistered retreat of academic privilege. Their influence, although ultimately far-reaching, has been mainly indirect. The average citizen has gone his habitual way, accepting his world and his religion uncritically, with naïve faith. In the nineteenth century all this was changed. The "temper of mind" which heretofore had been the prerogative of the few now became the characteristic of the many. "A new mentality was disclosed." [17]

It is not usually realized precisely how the gradual and largely unconscious initiation of the common man into the "scientific outlook" has altered his work-a-day attitudes. It has had its greatest influence at six points:

1. Through the enlarged Universe opened to the imagination of the ordinary layman by Modern Science—through the actual *facts of scientific discovery*. To be sure, as has so often been pointed out, Science has merely "pushed back" horizons which pre-scientific thinkers were already picturing in terms of incredible magnitudes. Indeed it is quite possible that our Universe in which, as Sir James Jeans described it, our planet is to be thought of as a minor satellite of one of the smaller stars which in turn is as one grain of sand among all the sea-sand on the earth—it is quite possible that that Universe is no more overpowering in its immensities, no more inconceivable in its intricacies, than was the heaven of Orion and the Pleiades to Job

17. A. N. Whitehead, *Science and the Modern World,* Macmillan, 1926, p. 122.

if we make allowance for the comparative intellectual maturity of educated minds in the two periods. But, it is now the common man who is introduced to the conceptions of the learned and feels his mind aghast before the world as Science portrays it. The result, undeniably, is a tendency toward mental confusion and bafflement. At the least, he feels a great gulf fixed between whatever Power may control so vast a cosmos and his puny life and petty concerns. At the worst, he discovers his mind taking refuge in a humble but resigned agnosticism. We are not here concerned to argue that this outcome represents a superficial analysis on the common man's part. We are concerned to recognize that that *is* the outcome.

2. Through the favorite rubric of scientific interpretation—*the concept of universal law.* The supreme goal of Science has been the unification of all knowledge within a single all-embracing system, and the uniform interpretation of all reality through a single all-sufficient principle of explanation—the principle of universal law. How absurd has sometimes been the resulting distortion of the facts may be indicated by a single illustration. In introducing his admirable discussion of *The New Psychology,* Mr. A. G. Tansley remarked that, if he were to try to develop a "science of mind," it was absolutely necessary for him to assume the fact of psychological determinism, that is, the complete control of mental processes by the law of mechanical causation. He gladly accepted the assumption and built his account of mind upon it. He further pointed out that this must be the invariable procedure of a psychology which claims the title of Science.[18] In other words, a Science which should be a systematic

18. "It is clear that if we are thus to recognize mind as a distinct subject of scientific investigation, the law of causation must hold within the psychic sphere, for without postulating the law of causation science is impossible. . . . Without the hypothesis of universal determination practical life would be impossible, physical science would be impossible and psychology would be impossible." A. G. Tansley, *op. cit.,* Dodd, Mead, 1920, p. 18. *Cp.* Joseph Needham, *The Great*

account of *facts* finds it necessary to read into its premises one of the theories which it is its duty, as Science, to weigh and pass judgment upon. Psychological determinism, instead of being a conclusion of its impartial investigation, is accepted as a presupposition of its inquiry. In the case in point, it welcomes an assumption which is decisively negated by the testimony of naïve experience and by an unforced reading of the facts to be interpreted. To be sure, this marks the surrender of a sound ideal for Science, but it has been prevalent scientific procedure. And it has made its imprint upon the plain man's thought. It has led to an overstress on continuity of development to the neglect of change, novelty and advance. It has exaggerated uniformities and slighted originality and individuality. Most important, it has encouraged men to conceive of the operation of all types of reality in terms of law, that is, in an analogy borrowed from the formal and impersonal procedure of human justice, or, more accurately, from the mechanical and sterile behavior of inanimate nature. In religion, the result, where it has not been a covert materialism, has been a depersonalization and devitalization of men's working thought of God.

3. Through the tendency of the scientific point-of-view to interpret everything as in the process of becoming. More specifically, through science's *emphasis upon evolution.* The concept of evolution has had a twofold and strangely paradoxical effect upon ordinary thought. It has created the impression of an "unfinished universe," of the world as still somehow in the making. In this aspect, it has focussed men's anticipations upon a future yet to appear, has presented the most serious difficulty for the traditional Christian claim of the pre-eminence of Jesus, and has encouraged the speculation that God himself may

Amphibium, Scribners, 1932, p. 30: "The principle of determinism can theoretically be dispensed with by the scientific worker, but in practice it never is. Some form of determinism must, for his purpose, hold good everywhere."

also be somehow still in the making.[19] In an unfinished universe where almost anything may yet happen, the common man finds the idea of an Eternal and Unchanging God both difficult and uncongenial. On the other hand, evolution has also stressed the all-controlling influence of origins. In this aspect, it has fixed men's attention upon the past, has tended to falsify historic perspective, and has encouraged the disposition to explain mature phenomena wholly by reference to their crude beginnings. It is sufficient commentary upon the confused state of Modern Thought that these two viewpoints proceeding from a single source are antipodal and quite irreconcilable; yet not infrequently they will be discovered comfortably domesticated within one mind's working philosophy.

4. The "scientific outlook" has exerted its impact also through the premium which Science places upon a certain class of truths arrived at in a certain way. This is the *"scientific method"* in the strict sense. The method is that of analysis, description, classification, generalization—the familiar technique of the laboratory. The truth supremely prized is that which can be caught in the meshes of this particular net—those facts which admit of complete analysis and description and which submit to classification as instances of a general type. Indeed so authoritative have these norms become that the common man tends to accept as "truth" only facts which satisfy their standards. It has not been sufficiently noted that by these tests, there are excluded from the province of "truth" not merely the more profound convictions of religion but, equally, the most cherished insights and certainties of the artist and the poet. In its century-long battle against this particular presupposition of the scientific outlook, religion has not struggled alone; its interests have been no less the concern of the poets, the

19. This strange view has been given serious defense in Professor S. Alexander's *Space, Time and Deity*. London, Macmillan, 1927. Also, apparently, by Professor Bergson in some of his later writings.

artists, the lovers, and the devotees of every aspect of human experience where worth attaches to richness and depth, to variety and originality and individuality.

In one of the most powerful passages in his great book, *Science and the Modern World,* Professor Whitehead pointed out how nearly the thought of the nineteenth century fell under the dominance of the dogmatic scientific assumptions of the period—mechanistic assumptions only recently discredited by Science itself. We were saved from that fate, he says, not by the arguments of the philosophers or the theologians (all too generally they bowed a servile knee or sought some facile reconciliation), but by the indomitable rebellion of the poets. The latter either could not or did not care to furbish their convictions with argument. They simply asserted their certainty that the scientific account was inadequate and delusive. They "knew in their bones" that the scientists were wrong. Theirs was an intuitive appeal to "naïve experience"—not to childlike and uncriticized experience, but to the richness and depth and variety and meaningfulness of human life before it had been forced within the straitjacket of *a priori* and artificial premises. Whitehead pays high tribute to Wordsworth in particular:

> "In the nineteenth century, some of the deeper thinkers among the theologians and philosophers were muddled thinkers. Their assent was claimed by incompatible doctrines; and their efforts at reconciliation produced inevitable confusion. . . .
>
> "Wordsworth in his whole being expresses a conscious reaction against the mentality . . . . [which] means nothing less than the acceptance of the scientific ideas at their full value. Wordsworth was not bothered by any intellectual antagonism. What moved him was moral repulsion. He felt that something had been left out, and that what had been left out comprised everything that was most important. . . .
>
> "Wordsworth alleges against science its absorption in abstractions.

His consistent theme is that the important facts of nature elude the scientific method. Berkeley, Wordsworth, Shelley, are representative of the intuitive refusal seriously to accept the abstract materialism of science. . . . The romantic reaction was a protest on behalf of value.

"I hold that the ultimate appeal is to naïve experience and that is why I lay such stress on the evidence of poetry."[20]

Dr. Joseph Needham, the eminent British biologist, set forth the same inadequacy of the "scientific outlook" in greater detail:

"Anyone who is at all intimate with the method of pure science realizes that its fundamental procedure of classification and indexing is the assertion of the abstract, the assertion of the group or class, and the absolute forgetting, at one and the same time, about the individual instances which have gone into the class. . . . Nothing can be more profoundly characteristic of the scientific method than its stern overlooking of the individual. Science is through and through statistical. . . . Even where the units do form unbreakable wholes, their individuality quickly disappears as they go through the mill of scientific treatment, issuing out as the sausage-like general law.

"All I want to insist upon in this connection is that we can trace a powerful influence of scientific abstraction on everyday life, an influence which is . . . fundamentally and bitterly opposed to the characteristic viewpoint of the religious spirit. . . . The habit of abstraction common to all scientific procedure weakens that attention to the individual and unique which always was and probably always will be an essential part of religion."[21]

5. Through the *scientific standards of truth* the "scientific outlook" has exercised great influence. If our comment upon the preceding effects of science has seemed unfavorable or critical, here we meet an invaluable gift of modern Science to the common man's outlook.

20. A. N. Whitehead, *op. cit.,* Chap. V.

21. Joseph Needham, *The Great Amphibium,* pp. 18–21.

And a challenge to Religion which Religion has been altogether too slow to acknowledge and answer. Ask the typical younger layman of today what it is which most attracts him in the great non-religious or anti-religious philosophies of the moment. He will reply it is their dogged determination to face facts, their unswerving fidelity to truth at whatever cost to wish or hope or dream, the modesty of their claims to knowledge, their preference for understatement rather than overstatement. Ask the same fair-minded critic of Religion the nub of his criticism. If quite honest, his reply will run somewhat as follows: "The principal vice of Religion is its subtle intellectual dishonesty and practical self-deception; it mistakes probabilities for certainties, beautiful hopes for stern realities; it thinks that it has accomplished great results simply because it enjoys the emotional sense of great strength; it claims to be on the path to high achievement merely because it has made profession of lofty goals; it is sincere but pitifully self-deceived, earnest but rather futile." He must be a self-assured Christian apologist who can stand up before such a penetrating indictment without misgiving and earnest searching of heart. Possibly this is the most valuable single gift of modern Science to our thought —a merciless insistence upon thorough-going intellectual honesty, coupled to the agnosticism of a healthy humility.

6. Finally, we confront Science's greatest impact upon the thought and life of the ordinary man, through its instrumental function in the creation of the Modern World, that is, through *scientific civilization.* Here we pass to the other great root of contemporary uncertainty in religion—the character of modern life.

It is not in the realm of his conscious outlook that we discover the most disastrous, as it is also the most pervasive, effect of the rise of Modern Science upon the common man's religious faith. It is in the area of his familiar daily life, through the fabric of industrial civilization.

Modern scientific civilization has tended to shut man off from living contact with his parent, the world of Nature—its immensities, its grandeurs, its austere indifference to him and his petty achievements, its beauties, its benefactions, its fascination; no longer can the "starry heavens above" give him their message. It has walled him within the artificial confines of a machine-dominated life and fostered in him an illusory security and self-sufficiency. It has herded him into vast impersonal aggregates of swarming humanity where he is debarred not only from contact with Nature but from the normal amenities of friendly association with his fellow-men. It has fixed his attention upon the amassing of things, the multiplication of accoutrements, the perfecting of appliances and conveniences. It has persuaded him that plumbing is more important than poetry, facts than understanding, the latest than the best, standardization than individuality, quantity output than originality, success than life. Its net result has been very materially to dull the modern man's awareness of religious reality, and to dissolve from his life the sense of need for religious certainty.

We have said that the embarrassment of contemporary Christian thought is to be traced principally to the joint impact of two forces—the dominant intellectual outlook of the past century and a half, and the practical consequences of the ascendancy of Science. In origin, these two influences were partly akin, partly different. In their development, they have pursued widely divergent courses, though from the outset their mutual interpenetration has been very great. In their final impact upon the religious life of our day they were one. That influence has been toward discrediting the knowability of Ultimate Reality, and the rigid limitation of proper materials for philosophy and theology to scientifically verified data of obvious experience. Contemporary uncertainty in religion was born of the critical sceptical outlook which Kant thrust upon the modern world; it has been suckled in the ease and worldliness of modern life. Men's minds were already tinged with scepticism about the validity of speculation; now they found their energies and interests drawn irresistibly into practical concerns where speculation seemed irrelevant and unreal. Increasingly, considerations of "Ultimate Reality" became foreign to their normal habits of thought which were intensely preoccupied with the manipulation of immediate reality—the stuff of this world and the march of passing events, concerning which it was superfluous to speculate. Did they not have all needed material for their philosophy of life within their immediate grasp?

It may seem that we have devoted disproportionate attention to the former of these two factors. But we shall view our problem in quite false perspective and miss altogether the significance of the modern scene unless we have clearly before us that other and companion factor which parallels and so largely controls the development of thought. In the larger view, it is very doubtful which of the two has actually had more important consequences for the destiny of Religion in our time. If modern scepticism began in theoretical uncertainty, it has been furthered by a practical non-concern.

While the dialogue between Science and Theology has continued through the Modern Period, it has been subject to sharp fluctuations, flow and ebb, of intensity. We can distinguish three major successive phases of that dialogue:

1). It was the late nineteenth-century findings of Darwin, Spencer, T. H. Huxley and their contemporaries which first forced the Christian mind to come to terms with the scientific description of our world. And it was the Christian interpretation of the truths of Science in the writings of John Fiske, Henry Drummond and others which brought relief and reassurance to those determined to be "intelligent moderns" as well as "serious Christians." This was accomplished principally through a radical dichotomy of knowledge into truths of

Nature, of fact, and truths of spirit, of value; and the assignment of exclusive authority for the former to Science, of the latter to Philosophy and/or Faith.

2). Again, in the early decades of this century, Science's renewed advance, especially in interpreting man, compelled a fresh effort of Theology. Again, Christian scientists demonstrated that the newer Science could enrich rather than contradict the Christian understanding of man. That both the physical and biological sciences are not without their positive and profound meanings for Christian Theology has been demonstrated again in the past few years by the extraordinary attention to a work widely hailed as the most important theological treatise of the last quarter-century, that of the remarkable Jesuit paleontologist, theologian and mystic, Pierre Teilhard de Chardin in his *The Phenomenon of Man* and other writings.

3). The dialogue will not down. Once again, today, Science is increasingly preoccupying men's minds as it is progressively dominating their lives. An eminent scientist recently issued a "Macedonian call" to Christian theologians to "come over and help us." [22] Once again, Christian Theology must make the fateful decision: will it venture forth into the mysteries of the newest Science and seek to establish contact between it and Christian Faith, so that Christians may live in this contemporary world as both "intelligent moderns" and "serious Christians." Or will it take refuge within a world-view—if you will, the "Biblical world-view"—formed before men knew the *truth* about the world in which men of today are fated to dwell, and thunder largely unintelligible and irrational "myths" which compel a dual, a divided, a schizophrenic existence? Here is one of the major challenges to Theology in our time. The issue is that with which we began: *fidelity to truth.*

22. Dean Harold K. Schilling of Pennsylvania State University, whose *Science and Religion: An Interpretation of Two Communities,* Scribners, 1962, has appeared since these pages were written.

If Liberal Theology is vulnerable to criticism for its attitude toward Modern Science, it is not because Liberal Theology insisted that men who are to live intelligently in the Modern World must come to grips with this force which, with each passing decade, moulds more and more decisively both men's thought and their lives, but because of a sometimes disproportionate attention to Science and because some liberal theologians harbored exaggerated expectations of the support which Science might bring to Christian Faith.

We have quoted the arresting insistence of Professor D. M. Baillie with respect to Liberal Theology's pivotal emphasis upon Jesus of Nazareth: "We can never go back to the pre-Jesus of History Christology." We may paraphrase Dr. Baillie's dictum and broaden its reference: "We can never go back to the pre-scientific, pre-Liberal, Theology."

Surrounding the confrontation of Science and Theology, however, there lies a much larger and more inclusive meeting of Christian Faith and the Modern Mind, of which the "outlook" fostered by Modern Science is a specific illustration. The authentic response of Christianity to that Mind and its attitude toward life and truth cannot be one merely of acceptance, adjustment and accommodation, but of radical criticism, challenge and correction. We have said earlier that the central intellectual issue for Liberal Theology is—*fidelity to Truth.* It is time to examine that issue in its wider context—the confrontation of Learning and Faith.

This confrontation marks the meeting-point of two of the most powerful and persistent concerns of the human spirit—the enterprise of *Learning* in its tireless quest for Truth in the conviction that it is Truth "which sets men free" and the heritage of *Religion* in its claim to the trusteeship, not of all truth to be sure, but certainly of the key to truth, the Christian Religion focussing upon One who is claimed to be not only the WAY and the LIFE but also, in some profound sense, the TRUTH.

However these two concerns—Learning and Religion—may differ, however far apart their paths may at times seem to diverge, they are at one in their joint allegiance to a single Sovereign—Truth. Moreover, it is obvious that if each rightly discerns that Sovereign and its claims upon them, they should discover themselves partners, yokemates in a common battle against ignorance and error.

To these general considerations, there is added a more immediate —what the current vernacular would delight to call a more "existential"—reason for taking this as a focus of our attention.

I have been much struck, and disturbed, by two recent, independent, comments on the state of religion in the U.S.A. by two distinguished and unusually discerning European observers. Both affirm the widely recognized "return" to religion. And then, both go on to voice a misgiving, essentially the same misgiving!

A brilliant young British philosopher, Professor John Hick, after a year on the Faculty of Cornell University, who immediately had a large influence among Cornell students, reported his discovery of a most surprising—in many ways, a most heartening—interest of American undergraduates in religion; and then confessed that there is one feature of this interest in religion which troubles him deeply: "students' almost total unconcern with the issue of truth."

And, perhaps the most perceptive and trustworthy European interpreter of the U.S.A. today, Professor D. W. Brogan of Cambridge University, summarizes his impression:

> "Religion in the U. S. A., like many things, is booming. . . . That there is a genuine religious revival, I do not doubt. That the churches are not in retreat, I do not doubt. I *do* doubt if the intellectual truce can be kept up indefinitely, in which few people dare to ask, 'Is this true?' "

"Almost total unconcern with the issue of truth;" "Few people dare ask, 'Is this true?' "

It is not easy to say exactly what it is which these two commentators, from entirely different points of view and on the basis of quite different observations, are pointing to. But that they are calling attention to something of real importance, few of us would question. At the least, they seem to be suggesting that, in all the immense and favorable attention to religion in these days, no one is troubling—Professor Brogan says "no one dares"—to force the question as to whether the Faith which is so widely proclaimed and accepted is really true, whether its affirmations are grounded in reality. Behind this disinterest in truth, beneath the surface, lies a hidden but debilitating, devastating and ultimately disastrous scepticism as to whether Christian Faith can stand up to rigorous scrutiny, can vindicate its beliefs as true.

Well; Dr. Brogan is certainly correct: if there be a truce between intellect and faith, between Learning and Religion, it cannot long continue.

How, then, shall we think of the confrontation of Learning and Faith? What should be their right relations? That that relationship has not always been one of easy and cordial partnership is obvious. Indeed, it is well to begin by recognizing that it must always be one of some tension, of strain. Not at all because Learning and Religion are basically incompatible, let alone contradictory. But because each carries at its heart always inadequacies, one-sidednesses, half-truths, to which the other is peculiarly sensitive, which it feels duty-bound to expose, which, ideally, it is its privilege to correct.

Learning, in this Modern Age, stands always under a three-fold temptation:

1. It is tempted to *excessive contemporaneity*. In its preoccupation

with new truths, its glorying in genuine, authentic truth freshly discovered, it is forever tempted to disregard, if not deny, ancient, no less authentic truth. This is the essence of *Modernism:* exaggerated confidence in the insights of the moment, disparagement of the wisdom of the Ages. Learning in this country in our day often tends to be the unwitting servant, when it is not the proud exponent, of Modernism. Upon the superficiality and distortion of mere contemporaneity, Religion stands in perpetual judgment. It not only declares the larger truth; it is itself a principal custodian and guardian of the Wisdom of the Ages. Moreover, so-called "new truth" is never as wholly "new," never as completely "true," as is claimed.

2. On the other hand, Learning is forever tempted to *premature finality*—to declare not only "This new truth is the only important truth," but also "This new truth is *all* truth." Both of these temptations are, of course, enormously aggravated by the fabulous, fantastic advance of Modern Science in its conquest of the secrets of Nature—in which broadly speaking, the latest is the truest. Over against this inadequacy, Faith should bring a two-fold corrective. First, as reminder of the currently neglected truth of Ages past, and also as prophet of the fuller truth of Ages yet to be. Not that FAITH itself has complete possession of that fuller TRUTH; not for a moment! But it should be alive to the larger Whole which forever surpasses and eludes man's grasp. Moreover its function is to remind the limited and partial perspectives of the moment of the incompleteness of all men's fumbling grasp on truth. But, it must be prepared to remind *itself* of that same truth about truth.

Faith's second corrective is at a far profounder, more significant level. Here, we are face-to-face with a dichotomy, a contrast, which runs like a persistent thread through the whole history of Modern Thought—variously defined as the contrast between FACTS and VALUES, between the OBJECTIVE and the SUBJECTIVE, between the realm of

NATURE and the realm of CHARACTER. It is a contrast, however you phrase it, which is perfectly obvious the moment one reflects upon man's life as every one of us knows it. Each one of us lives his life in two worlds at the same time, which Professor Hocking has distinguished as the realm of the "Public Order" and the sphere of the "Private Order." While these are in reality two concentric circles of a wider and narrower diameter at the heart of which each person stands, in experience they are rather more like two foci, between which our life moves back and forth as though within an ellipse which embraces them both. The wider circle, the first pole, the world of the "Public Order," defines one's life within his vocation, his community, his society, his nation, and the world. It is this fast-changing panorama of outward circumstance which gives life its movement, its novelty, its adventure; the "Public Order" is subject to change, advance, progress—where the latest, ideally, *is* the truest and best. At the same time, each of us lives within a "Private Order" of inner life, family, and intimate associations. There are the aspects of our human living which give it stability, beauty, deep satisfactions. Here, each man repeats the age-old pilgrimage of his predecessors in the story of the race. Here, not the newest but the best is Truth; the solons are not the latest scientists but the noblest saints. It is the "pure in heart" who know the Truth about life—the Truth that sets men free.

3. Again, Learning is forever tempted to an *exaggerated estimate of the powers of human intellect,* of reason alone, to discover and subdue all truth; that is to say—to intellectual pride and academic arrogance, one of the most subtle, self-delusive, spiritually debilitating temptations which lure and mislead the human spirit—the pre-eminent temptation of the scholar.

It is one of the functions of Faith to summon Learning to intellectual humility; to put scholarship in its place; and to do so, in part, by exposing the limitations of mere intellect, by insisting upon the wholeness of man—feeling and will, no less than mind—as alone adequate for the apprehension of truth.

But, let us not suppose that the service of criticism and correction is unilateral. Faith suffers its own distinctive temptations—temptations which Learning is peculiarly qualified to detect and expose:

1. The temptation to *anti-intellectualism,* the covert if not open distrust of the mind, suspicion of clear, honest, critical thinking, as inherently dangerous. Here, Learning summons Faith back to its own truer understanding of mind as, no less than feeling or will, a divine endowment; its own deeper confidence in God as Truth. As Coleridge once said: "He who loves Christianity better than truth will proceed by loving his own sect or church better than Christianity, and will end by loving himself more than all."

2. Secondly, the temptation to *obscurantism,* to uncritical traditionalism. For, if the standing vice of modern Learning is *Modernism,* that of Religion in every Age is *Traditionalism.* Religion does not present itself to this confrontation clean and pure, the perfect repository of truth. Its Faith is penetrated, permeated, and encrusted with superstition, as we have suggested earlier like an ancient vessel which, in the course of its age-long passage down the centuries, has accumulated barnacles without and refuse within. We repeat: from time to time, Religion requires to be dry-docked, scraped of its accretions, purged of dry-rot.

To this obscurantism, Learning brings the caustic, humiliating but fruitful catharsis of critical cleansing.

3. Once more, Faith is tempted to its own pride: *pride of soul* rather than of mind, spiritual rather than intellectual arrogance. If Learning often errs in its one-sided preference for understatement—affirming less of ultimate truth than man actually possesses, Faith is perpetually

guilty of the obverse vice—overconfident overstatement, pretense to more certitude than actually has been given it, exaggerated claims to knowledge of Ultimate Reality. Against this besetting sin of Faith, Learning brings the corrective of modesty in profession, spiritual humility.

This perennial, inescapable tension has its special contemporary expression, determined by the historical background of our immediate "existential" situation. That background may be briefly summarized as: glorification of Learning and disparagement of Faith, giving way to: distrust of Learning and resurgence of Faith.

It should hardly be necessary to recall that historic sequence. It is within the memory of many of us when Religion stood sore pressed, on the defensive, distrusted as to its truth-claims, discounted as to its social utility. Faith was branded an anachronism, a vestigial hangover from an earlier and less-enlightened period in man's evolutionary advance, a kind of vermiform appendix of man's intellectual life. How often we listened, in those so recent days, to Learning's funeral-dirge over Faith!

And yet, how long ago that day now seems—dim memories from an almost forgotten past. We have already moved into a New Day, a Day of disillusionment with the Gods of the Day that is gone. It would be an exaggeration to suggest that Learning is disparaged today; but its role as an all-sufficient interpreter of reality and guide for life is cast much more humbly.

Yet, sad to say, the Religion which seems on the way to become almost regnant is rapidly slipping into all the traditional vices from which, under the stern and stringent catharsis of Modern Knowledge, its most conscientious exponents were being purged:—distrust of intellect, of the mind's painful quest for knowledge; discount of the massive achievements of Modern Thought's prodigious labors; disdain of the issue of truth; uncritical proclamation of a tradition still burdened and corroded with the dead-weight of unexpurgated superstition—a superstition, once, it seemed, scotched, now reanimated in power; unjustified claims to more knowledge than it really possesses; unjustifiable and ultimately disastrous spiritual arrogance.

How long will this situation persist? How long can the issue of truth be evaded? It is in the setting of these questions that we turn to inquire: What, then, should be the distinctive contribution of Religion, especially the Christian Religion, to the discernment of Truth, such Truth as sets men free?

In the conviction of Christian Faith, what is truth?

The mere mention of the word "truth" inevitably suggests to our minds the meaning which we habitually associate with the term, the familiar dictionary definition: "agreement between statement and fact," such facts as Science especially masters.

If we are really to comprehend what the word means, as Christian Faith uses it, we must undertake the difficult mental discipline of divesting our thoughts of this conventional, accepted meaning, which we have inherited from the Greek philosophical tradition, and more immediately from the "scientific outlook." It comes to us in the Judeo-Christian tradition, this familiar word of five letters, worn thin and flat like a much-used coin through familiarity—freighted with the heritage of a long history of development in the thought of the Hebrew sages and prophets which lie behind the New Testament. We shall never really come to terms with its meaning unless we have some feeling for that inheritance. In Christian usage, it derived originally from a Hebrew word which means "to carry," "to support." Thence arose its richer meanings: Truth is—steadiness, uprightness, steadfastness, faithfulness—all of them, aspects of personal character, moral or ethical characteristics. And the source and ground of truth is One marked, above all, by these same qualities: trustworthiness, fidelity, constancy, God Himself.

Truth is no mere acquaintance with, description of, facts. It is apprehension of that which really is—of Reality. And that Reality, in Hebrew certainty is—God Himself—the Living Personal God; for Christian Faith—the God and Father of Jesus Christ.

Thus, to the haunting question of the Ages and the plaintive query of our own time: "What is Truth?," Christian Faith's answer is: "Christ is the Truth . . . He is Way, and Truth, and Life."

What does that mean? At least three things.

1. G. K. Chesterton with his fondness for paradox once said: "The only important thing about knowing the TRUTH is to know the really important truths." Most of the most important truths—what life's all about, its meaning, and its destiny—what is worth knowing and seeking and having (what the philosophers call "values"), what is a "good life," a "good marriage," a "good home," a "good career," almost all the really significant truths—in some profound sense, TRUTH itself—are personal, not only in the obvious sense that they concern persons and are known by persons, but also and therefore, that they can be made known, disclosed, only through persons.

Just here is the major limitation of servitude to merely scientific norms and methods. As Clutton-Brock once said of Marriage: "The man who treats his wife scientifically, i.e. as one of a class of wives, will never know much about marriage or about anything else worth knowing."

This is obvious common-sense; but its implications are far-reaching. It is FAITH's conviction that, because TRUTH, all the TRUTH that matters most, is grounded in the reality of a Living, Personal God, it is disclosed, made known to persons only through persons, fully only in a Person. If it is to furnish clear and sure guidance for human living, it must take flesh and dwell among us. Just that has in fact taken place in saints and seers of all Religions. Christian Faith declares that it has taken place supremely in Jesus Christ. "In Him was Life;

and that Life is the Light (i.e. TRUTH) for men." He is the TRUTH, because He is the LIFE—the very LIFE OF GOD in the life of a man.

2. More than that. Because the ground of all truth—God—is above all, righteous and holy, the most important truths are moral and spiritual. Yes; and for that reason, truth must be morally and spiritually discerned. There are preconditions for its discovery—preconditions of the same qualities as truth itself: uprightness, integrity, constancy, fidelity, steadfastness. Knowledge of truth is through moral and spiritual kinship with truth: "He who wills to do God's will shall know."

3. Lastly, there are not only preconditions, moral and spiritual preconditions, for truth's discovery. There are also consequences, moral and spiritual consequences. Because the deepest truths thus discerned by the mind and soul of man are profoundly ethical and spiritual, they demand response in kind from those to whom they are made known. Truth, by its very nature, lays down rigorous conditions for its discovery. By the same token, it places upon those who are privileged to enter within its presence demanding obligations—obligations of loyalty and obedience. They are primarily moral and spiritual obligations.

Here is the major word of Christian Faith to the world of Learning: the moral and spiritual preconditions and consequences of truth. As one interpreter has put it: "Truth does not appeal solely to the intellect. That it may be received, the moral dispositions of men must correspond with it; and its reception will further take effect upon character. If a certain moral attitude is a condition for receiving truth, so also, when received, it has profound moral effects. It makes free."

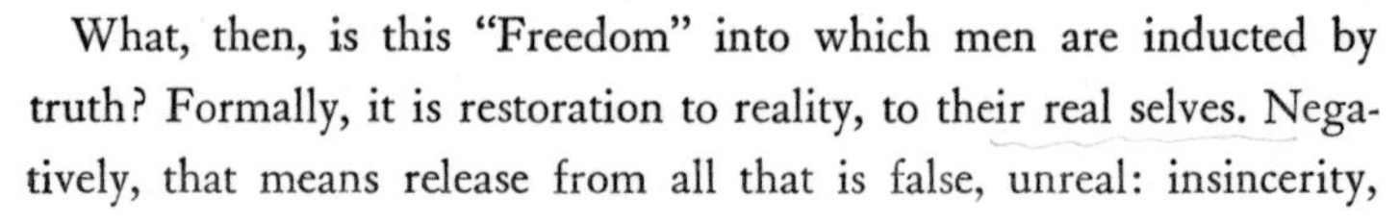

What, then, is this "Freedom" into which men are inducted by truth? Formally, it is restoration to reality, to their real selves. Negatively, that means release from all that is false, unreal: insincerity, duplicity, hypocrisy; but also fear, anxiety, self-preoccupation. Positively, it means kinship with Him who is Truth; glad obedience to His gracious command; surrender to His sovereignty, His service, which is perfect Freedom; participation in His Life, which is life indeed.

It may appear that we have devoted disproportionate space to the first charge against Liberal Theology; but it is the major indictment. The others may be dealt with very briefly.

b. Optimism Regarding Man and Social Progress

The charge that Liberal Theology has shared the Modern Mind's romantic *optimism regarding man's nature* and its *utopian expectations for social progress* strikes Liberalism in its most culpable frailty. Liberalism's sensitivity to the social demands of the Gospel and its reclamation of the claims of the Kingdom of God—its acceptance with dead seriousness of the petition that that Kingdom "come, on earth as it is in Heaven"—prepared the Liberal Mind for a too easy acceptance of Modernism's illusory hopes. Yet, even here, the authoritative spokesmen of the Social Gospel, notably Walter Rauschenbusch, understood the realities of human perversity and their outworking in both personal sin and social evil with a fullness and poignancy which have seldom been surpassed.

c. Moralism

The final count against Liberal Theology is *"Moralism."* If by that charge is meant Liberalism's sensitivity to and acceptance of the ethical demands of the Gospel, the charge must be acknowledged. But the response is not apology and surrender but reaffirmation and counteroffensive. Just here we are brought face-to-face with a patent weakness of Liberalism's critics and self-appointed successors.

At the heart of the so-called "return to religion" in our day, of which Neo-orthodoxy aspires to be the theological articulation, lies the most disturbing, confounding contradiction of the present moral and spiritual situation. Theological revival has been matched by no corresponding resurgence of morality. On the contrary, as theological interest has advanced, moral health in American life has steadily worsened.

It would be a mistake to attempt to establish a cause and effect relationship between theological resurgence and moral decline. Nevertheless, the two trends have moved parallel. Probably, the sounder reading of the facts is that, just as Liberalism too often shared the utopian confidence in man in the thought of the days of its birth so—and even more servilely—current Theology has accepted the contemporary mind's low estimate of man's moral capacities and responsibilities. More than that and more culpably., it has acquiesced and participated in contemporary man's muddy moral standards and casual moral practices. Indifference to ethical obligations, easy-going moral behavior which formerly were repented of as sin are currently rationalized as "natural." Proclamation of the universal burden of "original sin" is employed to justify carefree practice of specific sinfulness.

Liberal Theology's sensitive moral consciousness followed directly from a fresh confrontation with the ethical demands and expectations of Jesus' mind. Life which has lost living contact with that mind, which dismisses it as inaccessible or irrelevant, or which sets a chasm of discontinuity between that mind and the Object of Christian Faith, is all too readily absolved from its moral imperatives, all too easily acquiesces in practices which that mind would not tolerate.

2. DISCONTINUITY VS. CONTINUITY

Beneath these specific errors, in the contention of Liberal Theology's detractors, lies the presupposition which it shares with the Modern Mind, what Dr. Bennett had rightly identified as Liberal Theology's governing assumption: the assumption of continuity—"between revelation and natural religion, between Christianity and other religions, between the saved and the lost, between Christ and other men, between man and God." [23] So, likewise Dr. Cauthen: "The fundamental motif was the principle of continuity." [24]

What, then, is the basic presupposition of a correct and authentic Christian Theology, over against the falsities of Liberal Theology? The critic spells it out:

> "Discontinuity between the Christian revelation and all human and cultural attempts to discover the ultimate truth about human existence." "Discontinuity between faith and reason." "Discontinuity between God and the world, nature and man, and man and God." "Discontinuity between the human Jesus and the Divine Christ, the message of Jesus and the theology of the church about him." "Discontinuity between Christianity and all other religions." [25]

The alleged antithesis of "continuity" and "discontinuity," between which we are told we must choose, has been examined with such thoroughness by the most competent scientists, philosophers and theologians of the last generation that one would have supposed that the antithesis had long since been dissolved for minds of our day. What we actually confront throughout Reality as it is known to us is *neither* unqualified "continuity" on the one hand *nor* radical "discontinuity"

23. J. C. Bennett, *op. cit.*

24. Kenneth Cauthen, *The Impact of American Religious Liberalism,* Harper & Row, 1962, p. 232.

25. *Ibid.,* pp. 224, 230, 250, 251, etc.

on the other hand, but: *"Continuity of process and the emergence of real differences*—these are, in short, the twin aspects of the cosmic history." [26]

The Universe as we know it is not static. It is dynamic; it is continuously changing under our eyes. Moreover, that part of the Universe which we confront on this planet is the scene of a gradually but steadily advancing world-process—what we call *Evolution.* The story of our world is the history of slow but certain movement upward. Indeed, the one controlling conception which has emerged from the vast labors of recent workers in both Science and philosophy and which appears to claim the support of virtually all parties is the conception of an ascending series of levels or strata of reality, and of an age-long process of advance, from level to level.

Moreover, those who have studied it most authoritatively tell us that this process cannot be thought of in the figure of an unbroken incline plane, as though Nature had somehow boarded a cosmic escalator and was being automatically wafted upward. Rather, it must be thought of in the figure of a flight of stairs. Higher and higher types of being have, one after another, made their appearance—first of all, inanimate *matter,* with which the physical sciences of mathematics, physics and chemistry are equipped to deal; then, *life,* the sphere of the biological sciences; next, *mind,* the subject-matter of psychology and sociology; finally and climactically, what the philosophers of Evolution themselves usually denominate *"spirit."*

Thinking beings rise to the level of "spirit" when the motives of self-preservation, self-interest, self-gratification and self-advance give place to recognition of, response to, and devotion to ends which are entirely apart from and the denial of their own self-centered and selfish concerns—such ends as beauty and truth and goodness and

26. A. S. Pringle-Pattison, *The Idea of God in the Light of Recent Philosophy,* Oxford, 1920, p. 103 (italics his).

holiness and love—that is to say, when they give themselves unreservedly and wholly to those great and good things which we call "values."

No less an authority than the late Archbishop of Canterbury, William Temple, summarized this conclusion thus:

> "According to this view—and I think it is almost universally held, though the phrasing would vary from one exponent to another—reality exists in a series of strata of which it is sufficient to indicate the stages of matter, life, mind, and spirit. These are related to one another in such a way that the lower is necessary to the higher, but only fulfills its own destiny when the higher comes upon it and utilizes it, or, in the old phrase, 'informs' it."[27]

To be sure, the world-process is continuous, in the sense that we observe no sharp break at any point. But that is to tell but half the story. The fact of *continuity* must not blind us to the fact of *novelty*. The truth is that two characteristics have marked the cosmic-process from beginning to end—unbroken *continuity* and the emergence of the genuinely *new*.[28]

The Universe as far as we can apprehend it, then, is a vast, organic

27. *The Centrality of Christ,* Morehouse-Gorham, 1936, p. 64. For much fuller and more scholarly expositions by Temple, see his *Nature, Man, and God* and *Christ the Truth: an Essay.* (Macmillan, 1934 and 1924, respectively.)

28. Some such interpretation of Reality, with differences in detail to be sure, is to found in C. Lloyd Morgan, *Emergent Evolution* and *Life, Mind, and Spirit,* in J. S. Haldane, *The Sciences and Philosophy,* in R. F. A. Hoernle, *Matter, Life, Mind, and God,* in J. C. Smuts, *Holism,* and in Henri Bergson, *Creative Evolution,* as well as in the writings of a notable group of Christian theologians in addition to William Temple. Cf. my *The Plain Man Seeks for God,* pp. 94–106. Not the least striking and significant fact about the recently published thought of the great Jesuit paleontologist and mystic, Pierre Teilhard de Chardin, *The Phenomenon of Man,* etc., is that Teilhard arrived at closely parallel if not identical conclusions through his own entirely independent and solitary studies and reflection, apparently without any acquaintance with the works of the British scientists, philosophers and theologians just cited. Cf. Charles E. Raven's most recent book: *Teilhard de Chardin: Scientist and Seer.*

whole, made up of interrelated and interdependent types or levels of reality. As we seek to explain how it came to be so, we note further that our world is the outcome of a timeless process through which higher and higher types of reality have emerged from lower types, continue to rest upon the lower and more elementary types (*continuity*), and yet rise above those lower types and utilize them for their own needs and purposes. Finally, we observe that, high up the stair, there have developed, according to the familiar principle of emergence, new and quite different factors in the cosmic advance, creatures marked by a new characteristic. They are men and women distinguished by a sensitivity to, an interest in, a desire for, an urge to create and to serve things which cannot be measured and handled as inanimate matter is handled or even as biological life is handled—intellectual understanding, art, character, love, integrity, the vision of the ideal—utterly intangible but utterly priceless elements within human experience. These are things which Science can and should recognize, but which Science cannot measure and of which its methods can give no adequate account. And so the "scientific account" of the world is that of a process which produces as its highest terms emergent factors which are quite beyond the reach of Science. The cosmic history reports an agelong development which issues in the great and rich imponderables which lend life meaning, and in human beings who rise to the full stature of their humanity when they give themselves most completely in devotion to those imponderables.

There are many implications of such an understanding of Reality, with profound meanings for life and faith. It must suffice to point to only two:

1. This cosmic process which is continuous from the simplest items of *matter* to the noblest manifestations of *spirit* reaches its culmination on our planet in man. Not man as such, all men, mankind, however;

Evolution has gone far beyond that. The cosmic process reaches its climax, thus far, in a *certain type of man*—not the most brilliant intellectual or the shrewdest schemer or the dominating leader, but in persons who recognize most fully and respond most completely to the claim upon them of what we call values. But none of these great and good things can be brought into being save through human affection, loyalty, sacrifice, devotion, that is only as men voluntarily become their creators. Advance in the cosmic process is marked by increasing self-limitation on the part of the Creator, increasing freedom and participation by His creatures. The destiny of the creation, then—the destiny which signifies its ultimate meaning and in terms of which it must be interpreted—is that of the joining of man with God in the creation of a world-life of supreme beauty and goodness, the Kingdom of God. We are, by destiny, fellow-creators with God.

2. The highest level of Reality within our ken, then, is that of free, responsible, spiritual persons, accepting the claim of the highest upon them and giving to it their unstinting loyalty. Man stands at the summit of what we know of creation. And he who stands on the apex of that summit, proving not only the true destiny of mankind's life but also the true meaning of the whole creation, is one who surrenders himself utterly to the purpose which pervades it all. It is for that reason that the silent evidence of one human life may give clearer knowledge of ultimate truth than the speculations of the savants. That is why "the saint is the soundest theologian." This has been the conviction of the greatest religious spirits down the centuries—that the way to the knowledge of God and the understanding of life is not primarily through the brilliance of one's mind, but through the dedication of one's life and the depth of one's devotion to the highest. "He who wills to do God's will shall know."

Here, then, in such men—and supremely in the noblest of our humanity—is the clearest, most authoritative disclosure of the Power behind it all. It is for that reason, supremely, that the life and thought and work and faith and death and continuing influence of Jesus of Nazareth is our surest guide to the certainty of God. "He that hath seen him hath seen the Father." If the whole creation "groans and travails" to issue in him, if he is that "far-off, divine event to which the whole creation moves," then in him and through him we discern the Sovereign of Creation. To see him is to see that Sovereign. And, when in fact, we look upon him, we see his Father, the God and Father of our Lord Jesus Christ. Thus, an examination of the evidence presented to us by our world finally brings our attention to focus upon the fact of Jesus Christ.

What, then is the justification, the authority for the affirmations of discontinuity by Liberal Theology's critics? The answer is: The Bible. "The World of the Bible," "The Biblical World-view," "The Biblical Witness," "Biblical Theology"—these are the reiterated phrases to which appeal is made in the case against Liberal Theology. For, it is contended, the obverse of Liberal Theology's servitude to Modern Culture is its desertion of Christian Faith's true and only source and authority, in Biblical Revelation:

> "The Biblical way of viewing the divine-human encounter was obscured in liberal theology."
>
> "While the fundamental aim of liberalism was to harmonize the ancient Gospel with the life and thought of modern culture, the basic aim of post-liberal thought has been to discover the distinctive, authentic Christian faith which appears in the Bible."
>
> "The authority of the Bible will be put in the center of attention as the inspired and authentic witness to the mighty acts of God in history." [29]

The sound resolution of the antithesis between continuity and discontinuity in a general interpretation of Reality is:—neither unquali-

29. Cauthen, *op. cit.*, pp. 223, 225, 229.

fied continuity nor total discontinuity. Nature as it has emerged in Evolution is characterized by "continuity of process" and "the emergence of real differences." [30]

So, likewise, with most of the other realities and terms thrown in antithesis: faith and reason, revelation and natural religion, God and the world, nature and man, Christianity and other religions, Christ and other men, the message of Jesus and the theology of the church about him. In each case, what we actually confront is continuity with real differences. However, one of the alleged discontinuities Liberal Theology must emphatically disavow: discontinuity between the human Jesus and the divine Christ. It affirms one person—Jesus of Nazareth and the Living Christ, an organic unity, Jesus-Christ-in-the-life-of-the-world; here continuity is total.

Thus, we are brought to a final, the decisive issue: "The Centrality and Authority of Jesus Christ."

30. See, further, below, pp. 141ff.

CHAPTER FOUR

THE DECISIVE ISSUE:

The Centrality and Authority of Jesus Christ

CHAPTER FOUR

THE DECISIVE ISSUE:

The Centrality and Authority of Jesus Christ

Where, then, is the locus of Christian truth and authority?

Liberal Theology locates the decisive norm at one place: the mind and especially the faith of Jesus. We have said that Liberal Theology in each of its authentic expressions has been through and through Christocentric, indeed, that it has been the most determinedly and consistently Christocentric Theology in Christian history; and that its enduring significance rests upon the validity and adequacy of its interpretation of Jesus Christ. It is now time to subject that interpretation to careful and critical scrutiny.[1]

The moment we fasten attention upon the significance of Jesus Christ in Christianity, we are confronted by a puzzling paradox.

On the one hand, there has never been a moment of Christian history when Jesus Christ has been other than the determinative and authoritative center of authentic Christian Faith, both its life and

1. The pages which follow represent, in part, a reworking and extension of an earlier essay on "The Significance of Jesus Christ" in *Liberal Theology: An Appraisal*, pp. 205ff. (Copyright, 1942 by Charles Scribner's Sons.)

its thought. On the other hand there has been no time in Christian history when the mind of the Church has been more than imperfectly satisfied with its interpretation of this fact.

The centrality of Jesus Christ for Christian Faith can hardly be affirmed too categorically or too insistently. He has been, and is, in sheer fact, normative for both Christian experience and Christian conviction, for Christian belief no less than for Christian practice.

This was true from the outset. In its earliest proclamation, the Christian message was Christocentric if not strictly Christological. It was occupied almost exclusively with assertions of fact and expectation concerning Jesus Christ. Whether we attend to the reported speeches of Peter and his colleagues in Acts, or to Paul's account of his own public preaching, or to the didactic framework within which the Synoptic writers record their story, or to the underlying motif of the Fourth Gospel and the Epistle to the Hebrews, we meet a core of nearly identical proclamation (*kerygma*). It discloses kinship on the one hand with Jesus' initial public declarations as they are reported, and on the other hand with the crystallization of the Church's essential belief in its earliest generally accepted summary, the Apostles' Creed. Professor C. H. Dodd summarizes his investigation of *The Apostolic Preaching and Its Development* thus: "With all the diversity of the New Testament writings, they form a unity in their proclamation of the one Gospel" (p. 177). The first Christians had a single message for the world; it was a message of Jesus Christ.

What was true at the beginning has remained a constant feature of Christian Faith in its manifold and baffling variety through nineteen centuries. When the Christian Movement felt constrained to work out an authoritative formulation of its Faith, it was appropriate, indeed inevitable, that the issues of that formulation should center in Jesus Christ, that the earliest controversies should so prevailingly have focussed upon the interpretation of his being and meaning, that the one intolerable heresy should have been radically false views of him, and that the creeds should have been occupied so preponderantly with statements concerning Jesus Christ.[2] By a sure instinct, Christians of well-nigh every viewpoint sensed that what distinguished their Faith from others lay primarily in its assertions regarding Jesus Christ. They discovered that the persuasion of their evangel flowed from their presentation of him. They knew that the *raison d'être* of their Movement as well as its only effective cohesion lay in a united acknowledgment of Jesus Christ. Irresistibly the Church felt impelled to clarify its own mind concerning this pivotal reality, to present an intelligible apologetic to the world, to safeguard its unity, its purity and its power through fuller explication of his being and status. The wide divergences in emphasis and the mutual anathemas which seem to loom so large in the early history should not be allowed to disguise the larger fact: controversy was *within* a framework of common reference and assent—the centrality of Christ.

To be sure, the writings of the great theologians—Origen, Augustine, Aquinas, Calvin—might be held to be theocentric rather than Christocentric; their most original speculations lay in areas other than Christology. But the theologian himself would have been concerned to insist that the faith he declared had its focal center and its determinative principle in Jesus Christ, and that his own theology intended so to interpret it. Meantime, the living faith of the great bulk of Christians is best disclosed in the piety of the saints and in the Church's hymnody, always more trustworthy barometers of effective faith than formal theologies. It would be untrue to say that Christian

2. To be sure, these creeds placed preponderant stress on the birth and death of Jesus to the almost total neglect of his life. Cf. George S. Hendry, *The Gospel of the Incarnation,* Westminster, 1958.

devotion has been exclusively Christocentric. The strain of theocentric mysticism, for example, greatly strengthened by Neo-Platonism, has been prominent at every period. Overstatement of the facts encourages an underestimate of their significance. However, it is well within the facts to suggest that Christian piety has prevailingly centered in Jesus Christ. He has furnished its vitality and its norm.

The determinative significance of Jesus Christ is no less true of the Christian Movement in its length and breadth today. As one observes it widely across the earth, that Movement makes upon one many and diverse impressions. One impression overarches and overshadows all others. The Movement in almost every aspect has a single center—Jesus Christ. The *truth* which Christianity offers to the world is held in unity, as an arch by its keystone, through the *mind* of Jesus. The vast network of multitudinous and heterogeneous *undertakings* which the Movement is carrying forward in thousands of centers scattered widely in a hundred lands is inspired from a single source—the *spirit* of Jesus. The *living organism* of the Movement, distinguished by unique capacities for continuance, growth, expansion and adaptation, draws its seemingly inexhaustible vitality through its connection with *Jesus Christ.* Virtually everything which is most important derives from him and has its focus in him. This is the most obvious, as it is also the most important, fact to be noted about Christianity as a living reality in the contemporary world.[3]

It is impossible to define with completeness the meaning of Jesus Christ for the Christian Movement. Certain aspects of that meaning may be suggested:—

3. This point and the paragraphs which follow are further developed and illustrated in the writer's *For the Healing of the Nations: Impressions of Christianity Around the World,* Epilogue, Scribners, 1940.

1. *Jesus Christ is the instrument of Christianity's self-purification.* Here lies one of its most striking points of contrast with other religions. Almost without exception, they lack power to purge themselves of extraneous, spurious and cheapening elements. As they pass down the ages and amidst diverse cultures, they accumulate variegated accretions from foreign and inferior sources. These accretions work their way into the vitals of the religions and become part of their substance. Such truth and power as are native to them become so overlaid and interwoven with the tawdry and the vicious that they become seriously diluted and contaminated.

As we have observed earlier (pp. 29–30), Christianity has been subject to the same inescapable tendency toward perversion through accretion. How far such contamination may penetrate is all too patent. Yet, from the outset, Christianity has borne within its substance an agent for its own purification—Jesus Christ, especially the figure portrayed in the Gospels.

We discern it at work even in the first century when followers who came to their knowledge of the normative reality of the Faith through intimate companionship with Jesus began to be outnumbered and overbalanced by those whose initial experience was of the Living Christ, when ecstatic extravagances and exaggerated expectations imperilled the Church's permanence and usefulness. We have just referred to the essential *kerygma* common to all early Christian preaching, to which so much attention has latterly been directed. But to conceive of its pithy declarations as embodying the full Christian evangel would be to omit more than half of its content. That was only the public proclamation of the Faith. It aimed not to instruct but to convert. The street-corner preacher, in the first century as in the twentieth, is granted no opportunity to give his whole message; intuitively, he thrusts forth a few basic points, the most striking and arresting, best calculated to convict and convince. But if the listeners yielded to this strange yet strangely moving persuasion, they were drawn into the fellowship of followers. There, in the conversation and instruction of the *koinonia,* they came to know *who* it was "in whom they believed." There a very different evangel was being meditated, passed from mouth to mouth, and recorded for those who should come later. This, also, was a record of fact and event, an evangel of reminiscence—of Peter and Zaccheus and Mary Magdalene, of tales of a Good Samaritan and a Dissolute Son and a Grasping Debtor, of profound truth made simple and clear and compelling in stories and figures and vivid incidents, above all of the words, deeds, thoughts of the Person in whom their new Faith centered. The portrait of the historic figure began to work its ever-repeated transformation—exposing absurdities, chastening excesses, sifting truth from fancy and reality from magic, purifying crude and false notions, correcting sincere but misguided misinterpretations of him, stirring imagination, quickening faith, chastening infidelity, training a devotion both more intelligent and more unalterable.

We see it even more clearly in the second and following centuries when direct contact with the framework of Judaism and with the source-springs of the Faith was severed and the Christian Movement rushed headlong, like a torrent loosed from restraining banks, out amidst the demoralizing paganisms of the Graeco-Roman world. One factor principally saved Christianity for enduring significance. The words and deeds and faith attributed to Jesus of Nazareth had by now won permanent preservation within the Gospels. Feeling its way amidst the labyrinthine complexities of philosophical speculation in that contentious and befuddled world, the Christian mind maintained its sense of direction by keeping firm grip upon its pivotal certainty—the centrality of Jesus Christ. All the while that its overt concern was to make its Faith intelligible in the diverse thought-forms of contemporary usage, that Reality was holding the varied interpretations within a corpus of common reference, and thereby preserving the unity of the Movement.

Something of the same process may be discerned quietly at work through the whole of Christian history. As already remarked, it has found less ready channels in the systems of the theologians than in the preaching of the prophets and the psalmody of the saints. Yet only a superficial reading of the theologians misses its pervasive power; although here, again, it exerted its influence more largely through their exhortations and private devotions than through their dogmatic formulations—through Clement's hymns rather than the *Stromateis,* through Origen's exegesis rather than the *De Principiis,* through Augustine's sermons rather than the *Enchiridion,* through Aquinas' personal piety rather than the *Summas.*

The fact to which we are pointing becomes most obvious and most important when contact with an unfamiliar culture or a newly emergent dogmatism threatens distortion and betrayal of essential Christian Faith. Never more clearly than in Christianity's outreach amidst foreign religions and cultures. In these latter years, for Christians in many lands where association with the corrective influence of the world Church has been well-nigh dissolved, e.g. beyond the several "curtains," it is Jesus Christ and he almost unaided who must fight the battle within their souls against the menacing forces which would lure them from truth and the Kingdom.

Through the records of the New Testament, the Figure there portrayed ever afresh lays constraint upon his Movement in the world, impelling it to new advances. This is the principal secret of Christianity's continuity, its authority, its unique capacity for endless self-renewal.

2. *Jesus Christ is the agent of Christianity's life-claiming and life-transforming influence.*

This, likewise, was true from the beginning. Paul's experience was not unrepresentative. Whatever the authenticity of the account of his confrontation with Jesus on the Damascus Road [4] or however we account for Paul's "conversion," it is a truism that what altered a chief persecutor into the foremost advocate was a new apprehension of Jesus Christ. And Paul's education in effective evangelism is revealed in the contrast between the reported Sermon on Mars Hill,[5] attempting to build toward Christian truth from a broad base of universal religion and natural theology until his assertion of the resurrection prompted his hearers to scorn, *and* his avowed tactics at Corinth—"I determined when among you to know nothing except Jesus Christ, and Jesus Christ the crucified—to Jews, an offense; to Gentiles, sheer nonsense." [6]

Here also, what was true at the outset has prevailed through the centuries since. Today it is almost unfailingly the case wherever Christianity exhibits impressive vitality and amongst whatever types of adherents. Again, it is where Christian Faith makes its way among those previously wholly outside its acquaintance that the deeper secret of its influence is most clearly disclosed. A single illustration must suffice. Here is the statement of an able young Chinese scholar widely known in literary circles:—

> "In spite of difficulties, I was brought into Christianity. I was simply captured by Christ! I became a Christian, not by persuasion of any doctrine, not by the prudent calculation of the superiority of Christianity as a religion, not even by the certainty of a personal God.
>
> "One evening, eighteen years ago, I was in the home of a missionary. For the first time I read the 'Sermon on the Mount'. I never

4. Acts 9:1–8, 22:4–11, 26:11–20.

5. Acts 17:16–33.

6. I Corinthians 2:1–5.

knew there was such a thing as the 'Sermon on the Mount' before.

"But now, for the first time, I read the 'Sermon on the Mount'. And then I saw a figure. It was solemn, yet full of sympathy; it was penetrating, yet lovable. It stirred my heart with an indescribable warmth, but it also imparted a peace I had never known. I went back to my room, but I could not sleep. I had found something, and I was too full of the new discovery to lie down to rest . . . Even now I cannot describe in so many words what the discovery was. The only thing I knew was that every word of the Sermon pierced into my heart and spoke to my condition. I knelt down and said, 'Lord, Thou art my Lord'. . . . ."

Alongside of this testimony from a young Chinese whose initial contact with Jesus Christ came through the pages of the Gospels picked up by chance from a guest table in a missionary's home, we may place the witness of another whose life likewise was given almost wholly to China, born in China though not a Chinese but a son of American missionary parents, not a non-Christian but a Christian by birth and heritage. To all who knew him, John Leighton Stuart has been one of the noblest and most useful Christian statesmen of our day and a Christian saint. After half a century of service to higher education of the Chinese, he was nominated by General George C. Marshall to be the last American Ambassador to China before its National Government was driven from the Mainland; of him General Marshall said, "It is the man, the character and the general range of his experience which appealed to me." Revealing the sources of his dedication and the secret of his faith as these were formed in youth, John Leighton Stuart wrote:

"Jesus Christ became an adored Master and ideal object of a young man's enthusiastic devotion, instead of being primarily a theological doctrine about whose mysteriously sublime nature and attributes it was heretical to have any doubts. . . . . This fresh and fascinating appreciation of Jesus . . . . became then and still is the essence of my religious faith. It has remained undimmed and free from all disillusionment after all the experiences and altered theological views of these intervening years." [7]

Reared in a traditional Southern Presbyterian environment, Leighton Stuart's kinship of spirit with the outlook of Liberal Theology is indicated in his hope for a new interpretation of Christian Faith appropriate and adequate to the needs of today:

"Christianity inevitably brought to China its traditional creeds and theological formulations. I have for a long time hoped that Chinese theologians might give some fresh and creative interpretations of Christian truth to their own people and to the world. It may be that the ordeal through which the Chinese Church is now passing will so enrich and deepen the religious experience of their Christian thinkers that what we have longed for may more quickly be realized, just as the most profound spiritual insights of the Old Testament came in the literature written after the Exile. China's history, philosophy, and indeed all of its best literature is primarily concerned with the moral relationships of people to one another. Certainly out of such a great tradition, challenged and sifted in the fierce overturning of these years, and vitalized by Christian truths that have taken deep root in Chinese thought should come fresh illuminations upon the meaning of Jesus Christ for our human race." [8]

As his life drew toward its close, he reiterated its foundation and its center:

"Jesus Christ is as sublimely satisfying to me in my old age as he was in my youth. He has my absolute reverence and devotion. His life, teaching, death and resurrection form a harmonious whole. His crucifixion reveals the ultimate in faith and love." [9]

7. John Leighton Stuart, *Fifty Years in China*, Random House, copyright 1954, p. 26.

8. *Ibid.*, pp. 298–99.

9. *Ibid.*, p. 300.

When the Jerusalem Conference of 1928 prefaced its findings with the statement, "Our message is Jesus Christ," to many it seemed a pious platitude without a clear or vital relevance. Actually it was a simple declaration of the one common and effective proclamation of Christian Faith.

3. *Jesus Christ is the inspirer of Christianity's extension and prophetic outreach into untouched areas of the earth's surface and, equally, into unredeemed aspects of the world's life.*

Virtually every great renewal of vitality within Christian history has accounted for itself as a "return to Jesus Christ."

But as Dr. Charles W. Gilkey has reminded us, every movement "back to Jesus" has discovered itself transformed into a movement "forward with Jesus." Fresh contact with the historic figure, his mind and faith and fidelity, impels those who allow themselves to come within range of its disturbing ferment to launch forth on new adventures and crusades in behalf of mankind's relief and advance.

4. *Jesus Christ is both the prompter of and the basis for Christian unity.*

That becomes very clear to anyone who attends a great world gathering of Christians in their diversity of traditions, viewpoints and practices. One quickly discerns that the assemblage has one and only one center; their common loyalty to Jesus Christ is the basis of their unity. Ecumenical faith is preeminently faith in Jesus Christ. Those who drew the specifications for the World Council of Churches were guided by a sound instinct in proposing as its basis merely the acceptance of "our Lord Jesus Christ as God and Saviour." Many devout Christians would have preferred the alteration of a single word to bring the formula into fuller conformity with the words of Scripture and of customary phraseology: "Lord and Saviour" rather than "God and Saviour."[10] But it has the merit of grounding squarely upon that which is focal and universal for all Christians.

Jesus Christ is not only the common standing-ground upon which alone Christian unity may hopefully be founded. He is himself the principal stimulus toward its realization. It is noteworthy that sensitiveness to what is believed to be his desire and response to it are strongest among Christians of the Younger Churches who are resolved "to put an end to the scandalous effects of our divisions" and to advance "in the path of union."

5. *Jesus Christ is,* supremely, *the one who bestows God,* both the knowledge of what and who God is, and the faith by which men may trust in Him.

It is an eminent Jewish scholar, Dr. Solomon B. Freehof, who declares:

> "The consciousness of the presence of God has come to millions of men and women through Jesus . . . He is still the living comrade of countless lives. No Moslem ever sings, 'Mohammed, lover of my soul,' nor does any Jew say of Moses, the Teacher, 'I need thee every hour' . . . . . Jesus brought God near to men through His presence. He makes the Divine personal for myriads of worshippers."

Christianity's power to win the allegiance of mankind rests finally in its grip on truth. The core of its claim to truth is its certainty of God. The God of that certainty is the God and Father of Jesus Christ, the God in whom Jesus himself trusted.

Moreover, Christians' certainty of God, their reliance upon Him, is

10. At the Third Assembly of the World Council at New Delhi in 1961, this Basis was slightly revised and expanded, and now reads: "The World Council of Churches is a fellowship of Churches which *confess the* Lord Jesus Christ as God and Saviour *according to the Scriptures, and therefore seek to fulfill together their common calling to the glory of God, Father, Son, and Holy Spirit."* (Alterations and additions are italicized.)

possible for them only through their trust in Jesus' faith in Him. That is not a bad definition of the heart of Christian Faith: Christian Faith is, basically and finally, faith in the faith of Jesus of Nazareth. It is confidence in, and utter commitment to, the assumptions about life, the convictions regarding Reality, above all the certitude of the Living God which constituted Jesus' faith; it is trust in Him in Whom Jesus trusted utterly. Such faith in the God and Father of Jesus Christ becomes possible for us by virtue of Jesus' trust in Him. Such faith is, quite literally, "through Jesus Christ, our Lord."

It is not difficult to suggest what Jesus Christ means—indeed, always has meant—as simple matter of fact for the thought and life of Christians. When we turn to the attempts to interpret that fact, the other side of the paradox appears. At no time in the Christian centuries has the mind of the Church been more than imperfectly and provisionally satisfied with its explanation of this central reality.

It would be an exaggeration to say, as has been done, that "there has never been a 'Doctrine of the Person of Christ' to which great numbers of Christians have given assent which has been other than a thing of patches and compromises, hiding beneath sonorous phrases, unresolved inconsistencies and contradictions." But there is sufficient truth in this harsh generalization to give it disquieting point. Assent to the formula of Nicaea, the Church's first attempt seriously to define its explanation of Jesus Christ, hardly outlasted the benediction which dispersed the Council. Nine years later, the Council of Tyre, although not formally abrogating Nicaea's creed, reversed its decisions. While the mind of the Church ultimately came to agreement in a reaffirmation of the Nicaean phrases, they can hardly be said to have furnished an undisturbed resting point. As with all of the Christological formularies, the Niceno-Constantinopolitan Creed is more a definition of the problem than its solution.

We have earlier noted that the tortuous and difficult development achieved climactic and characteristic expression, appropriately, in the last of the great creedal declarations, that of Chalcedon. It is unnecessary to repeat here the obscurities and seeming self-contradictions of that statement.[11] As we observed, the Sixth Council of Constantinople in 680 carried the dominant line of development to its *reductio ad absurdum* in the unblushing affirmation that Christ had two wills and two energies fully operative—still the definitive formulation of orthodox Christology.

We repeat: the upshot of six centuries of uninterrupted effort toward an adequate interpretation of Jesus Christ is well summarized by Reinhold Seeberg: "What this Christology handed over to the Church was not a finished result but a problem—that God Himself should have lived and walked here, a man like to us." [12] This was precisely the problem posited from the outset.

The comparative moratorium in Christological controversy from Constantinople to the eve of the Reformation should mislead no one. Nor should the relative similarity in the Christologies of the great systematizers as they reproduced, on the whole faithfully, the creedal positions. Seeberg's characterization continues apt. Nor can it be said that later interpretations have better succeeded in satisfying the mind of the Church—the more religious interpretations of the Reformers, or the more rationalistic interpretations of the radicals, or the (to us) more intelligible interpretations of the moderns since Schleiermacher. Indeed the Church in the large has continued loyal to the so-called "ecumenical creeds."

The dominant impression from even so cursory a survey of the place of Jesus Christ in Christian Faith may be summarized thus: in the Church's central conviction, its certainty from which all others

11. See, above, pp. 32–33.

12. *Lehrbuch d. Dogmengeschichte,* A. Deichert, 1895, i, 231.

flow and upon which they hang, the Church has been utterly satisfied in its soul; it has never achieved an explanation which has satisfied its own mind, let alone the more critical minds of inquirers and scoffers.

The reason for this paradox is familiar. It does not spring from uncertainty as to what the Church feels compelled to declare concerning this central Reality. There has been no serious doubt or division on that crucial point. Virtually from the first, Christians of all persuasions and parties have asserted with a single voice:—"*Jesus Christ was at once truly a man, and yet also uniquely God in human flesh.*" The paradox arises from the fact that the Church has never succeeded in discovering an intellectual framework and categories of interpretation within which its unhesitating and unanimous affirmation might be brought into intelligible relation to the corpus of general knowledge, and thus made persuasive to the non-Christian mind.

Do we find ourselves in a happier situation? Does the contemporary scene offer better promise of a satisfactory explanation? In view of the failures of history, bold indeed would be the hope that the mind of our time will wholly succeed. We shall attempt no restatement of the "Doctrine of the Person of Christ," but rather answers to three questions which may furnish guide posts for our understanding of Jesus Christ:

1. *What* IS *the central reality of Christian Faith—the fact of Jesus Christ?*
2. *Can the Church's affirmation concerning this reality be made intelligible and convincing to the mind of today?*
3. *What is the nature of Jesus' authority for our thought and life?*

1. *The fact of Jesus Christ,* the determinative center of Christian Faith, both its belief and its practice, is—*the total impact of Jesus Christ*

upon history. That fact embraces various and successive phases of a single organic personal reality—*Jesus-Christ-in-the-life-of-the-world.* The Reality which we actually confront, and which we seek more fully to comprehend and more adequately to interpret, is not merely the human career of a certain man who traversed the roads of Palestine in the days of the Caesars. Nor is it a unique supernatural event occurring through the life and death and resurrection of a misty, mythical figure who trod the earth in the semblance of a man. Nor is it a stream of influence in history initiated somehow by that life or by events connected with it and then pursuing a more or less independent course down the ages. Rather it is a continuous, coherent, consistent personal reality, rooted in and springing from a particular commanding human life, and persisting with powerful effectiveness through nineteen centuries. The historic career and the influence following cannot be set in antithesis or even in contrast. They are an organic whole. Here continuity is at a maximum, total. Neither can be understood apart from the other. Strictly, neither can rightly be thought of apart from the other. The conception of either is authentic only as it necessarily involves the other. In fact, each furnishes to the other something of a norm by which it may be distinguished from myth and fable and extravagance. The Christ of the centuries reveals the *power* of that reality. Only in view of what Jesus became to men after his death, what indeed he already was to those who troubled to record his life, and of all that issued and still issues from his continuing influence can the human life be read aright and truly interpreted. But Jesus of Nazareth defines the *authenticity* of that reality. The Christ of Christian history and of present experience should never be thought of except through the clear lineaments of the words, deeds, mind, spirit, faith of the man, Jesus of Nazareth. All that *is* truly Christ is unmistakably continuous with that life. All else is secondary and dubious accretion.

This was the view of the New Testament:

> "The Jesus of History is valueless and unintelligible unless He be experienced and confessed by faith as the living Christ. But, if we would be true to the New Testament, we must at once reverse this judgment. The Christ of faith has no existence, is mere noise and smoke, apart from the reality of the Jesus of History. These two are utterly inseparable in the New Testament. They cannot even be thought of apart. There is no word about Christ which is not referred to Him who suffered under Pontius Pilate, and which is not at the same time intended as the Gospel applicable to all men of every time and in every place. Anyone who attempts first to separate the two and then to describe only one of them has nothing in common with the New Testament."[13]

The view of the New Testament has guided authentic Christian Faith always. As Canon Hodgson has said, "The Gospels, if not the starting-point, are the touchstone of Christological theory, and we must always test ourselves by asking whether we can recognize the Christ of our thought in the Christ of history."[14] The only Christ whom Christianity knows is one who is at every point the direct continuant of Jesus of Nazareth.

Yes; but can we have trustworthy knowledge of Jesus of Nazareth? And how important is such knowledge for Christian Faith? Under the influence of a powerful, some would say the dominant, school of New Testament scholarship, there is some disposition to claim that the words and acts, the mind and faith of Jesus are not important. In any event, we must dispense with them since we can never know him. Thus, one of the foremost Christian scholars of our day in a popular volume of very wide reading declares:

13. Gerhard Kittel, in *Mysterium Christi,* ed. G. K. A. Bell and D. Adolf Deissmann, London, Longmans, Green, 1930, p. 49.

14. Leonard Hodgson, *And Was Made Man,* Longmans, 1928, p. 4.

> "At the source of Christianity in Palestine there was a very remarkable and attractive personality of some kind, but all imaginative reconstructions of that personality based upon our fragmentary data must be highly conjectural. . . .
>
> "As a figure calculated to inspire men to heroic acts of self-sacrifice, it may be doubted whether the figure of Jesus, if detached from what Christians have believed about him, is adequate."[15]

Upon the wisdom of some scholars, sometimes even those of great eminence, one is tempted to bring Masefield's stinging indictment:

> "The trained mind outs the upright soul,
> As Jesus said the trained mind might,
> Being wiser than the sons of light.
> But trained men's minds are spread so thin
> They let all sorts of darkness in;
> Whatever truth man finds, they doubt it.
> They love, not truth, but talk about it."[16]

Just here, we come hard up against the gravest, ultimately the most decisive challenge to Liberal Theology. Yes; but not merely to a particular Theology. Here is a challenge which strikes at the very heart of Christian Faith itself. If it should prevail, it would dissolve that center and leave the Faith bereft of its indispensable keystone.

This is the scepticism being pressed by the more radical contemporary New Testament scholars. Its determinative importance for the future of Christianity can hardly be exaggerated. I shall be bold to venture this forecast: history will judge that, in our day, the crucial issue for Christianity was being determined, not in its confrontation with the secular world or with renascent other Religions, nor in the fulfillment of Christian Unity, but within Christian scholarship—at its very center, its fulcrum, upon which all else turns: the clarity and

15. Edwyn Bevan, *Christianity,* Holt, 1932, pp. 242, 239.

16. "The Everlasting Mercy," The Macmillan Company.

surety of its apprehension of, the firmness of its hold upon, Jesus; or, more accurately, of his grip upon it.

There is neither space nor need to review the all too familiar current uncertainties about our knowledge of Jesus. Adequately to report and assess them would require a volume in itself. One may be permitted the *obiter dictum* that he has delved into the alleged grounds for the scepticism in their most authoritative presentations, and has emerged unconvinced. We cited earlier Whitehead's devastating judgment on the nineteenth-century theologians who bowed a too ready and servile knee to the then-prevailing scientific materialism: "In the nineteenth century, some of the deeper thinkers among theologians and philosophers were muddled thinkers." [17] In the longer and sounder perspective of decades, some of these nineteenth-century thinkers now appear absurd, even pathetic, in their servility to a false Science. I shall risk a response of indignation and scorn to prophesy that, in the longer and truer perspective of decades hence, no small part of the dominant current New Testament interpretation will appear tragically distorted, yes pathetic; some of its scholars, "muddled thinkers."

The present position within New Testament scholarship with respect to trustworthy knowledge of Jesus has recently been set forth by two of my colleagues in volumes which have come from the press while these pages were in process of final revision.

Dr. W. D. Davies, in an essay in a volume of tribute to Dr. Oscar Cullmann, summarizes the situation thus: [18]

> "The question of the origin and transmission of the tradition of the works and words of Jesus has recently especially occupied New Testament scholars and theologians. . . . The main answers that

17. A. N. Whitehead, *Science and the Modern World,* Macmillan, 1927, Ch. V. See, above, pp. 65–66.

18. W. D. Davies, "Reflections on a Scandinavian Approach to 'The Gospel Tradition,'" in *Neotestamentica et Patristica,* Leiden, E. J. Brill, 1962, p. 14.

have hitherto been given to it . . . . are three: 1) That which separates Jesus of Nazareth radically from his world and time and finds in the tradition presented in the New Testament a misunderstanding of Him, born of 'Qumranizing' and 'Judaizing' tendencies in the primitive Church; 2) That which derives that tradition mainly from the primitive communities which created and formed it to meet its own needs. On this view the tradition is from the Church, by the Church, for the Church: it reveals primarily, not Jesus of Nazareth, but the Faith of the Church in Him, and the degree to which He is represented or can be discovered through the Gospels is testily and variously assessed; 3) That which finds the origin of the tradition in the life, teaching, death and Resurrection of Jesus Himself, as these were remembered and preserved by the Church. The tradition was not created by the latter and, although in the course of its preservation and transmission it could not but be modified, it was never wholely subservient to the needs of the community but remained true to its initial impulse in Jesus Himself. Thus, on this view, however much they represent the Church, the Gospels preserve the authentic figure of Jesus of Nazareth, whose act we can see and voice hear in them."

Dr. John Knox declares:

"New Testament scholarship has for a generation been saying in effect: What we have in the New Testament is a record and reflection of the life and thought of the early Church. This is as true of the Gospels as of the Epistles. What confronts us immediately and directly in the New Testament documents is simply and only the primitive community—what it remembered, what it knew, what it thought, what it felt." [19]

Dr. Knox cites "Rudolf Bultmann's extreme skepticism as to the possibility of our recovering the content of Jesus' career—and his

19. John Knox, *The Church and the Reality of Christ,* Harper & Row, 1962, p. 9.

disparagement of the importance of our doing so even if we could,"[20] and adds:

> "In a word, skepticism concerning what can be known about the so-called historical Jesus has been widely current in the Church for a generation or more; and although fashions in biblical criticism, like fashions generally, often change, and conservative trends from time to time take over for a while, this skepticism is bound to persist so long as men's minds are free; the grounds for it are too extensive and too real."[21]

As to his own view, Dr. Knox asserts:

> "I have always felt that I belong at this point among the 'conservatives'—that is, ... I see no reason to doubt that the Gospels bring us a great deal of authentic information about Jesus. . . . I believe that the picture of an actual historical person emerges in the Gospels and that this picture is to a large extent trustworthy. As regards our present problem, however, differences among us in respect to this matter are irrelevant. Once we recognize the character of the Gospels as 'Church books', in which such facts about Jesus as they contain can be found only in or under records and reflections of the later Church's interests, needs, and convictions (so that the critical tools of the historian are needed to identify them)—once this happens, we open the door to the indicated question, no matter how comparatively 'conservative' our position may be."[22]

That is to say, while he himself apparently does not accept the more negative assumptions of the "extreme scepticism" as to the possibility of our knowing Jesus, his discussion proceeds without challenging or refuting those assumptions.

To be sure, at the present moment, there is a slight pendulum swing away from the more extreme sceptical conclusions of Rudolf

20. *Ibid.*, p. 14.

21. *Ibid.*, p. 15.

22. *Ibid.*, pp. 15–16n.

Bultmann and his faithful followers in the direction of a "new quest for the historical Jesus." A summons to this "quest" has been sounded by, among others, my colleague, Professor W. D. Davies, in his Inaugural Lecture as Edward Robinson Professor of Biblical Theology at Union Theological Seminary.[23] However, this retreat from inordinate scepticism is, for the most part, being carried on by disciples of Professor Bultmann and from such an extreme limit of the pendulum that it thus far appears to offer meagre prospect of restoring our knowledge of Jesus to its true center.

Dr. Amos Wilder, one of the ablest and most respected of contemporary American New Testament scholars, has put the issue thus:

> "The Man Christ Jesus preached by the neo-orthodox is a kind of symbol 'X', an unknown quantity. . . . . The son of Joseph was no 'X', nor an icon in a niche, nor a Kierkegaard in advance of his time. He was a real protagonist in a human situation. He was a political and religious figure, calling to repentance, challenging corrupt institutions and authorities and expressing compassion toward the neglected and victimized of his day." [24]

In the meantime, the ordinary Christian and the great bulk of Christian preachers and even teachers continue to proceed on the assumption which has guided the Church across the centuries, that the portrait of Jesus in the Gospels is substantially authentic. As, indeed, they must. For, if the sceptical assumptions which Dr. Knox suggests are axiomatic for New Testament scholarship should prevail and be accepted and implemented in Christian preaching and piety, a large proportion of church sermons will have been shorn of their Scriptural bases, a large part of private devotion of its presuppositions and guidelines. Nothing less than that is at stake in

23. "A Quest to be Resumed in New Testament Studies" in *Christian Origins and Judaism,* Ch. I.

24. Amos Wilder, *Otherworldliness and the New Testament,* SCM Press, 1955, pp. 80, 83, 84.

the resolution of the widely spreading uncertainty over the trustworthiness of our knowledge of Jesus.

If Christian Faith is henceforth to be bereft of what has always been in principle its determinative and regulative norm, what has been in fact, as we have reminded ourselves, its source of both power and self-correction in individuals and movements which have most authentically and worthily represented Christianity in the world across the centuries—the historic reality of Jesus Christ, especially as defined in the Figure portrayed in the Gospels—at once the question presses: where, then, is the locus of Christian truth and authority? In general, two alternative answers to that crucial question are proposed.

Some Christian scholars, both Biblical and systematic theologians, reply, as we earlier reported: in "the Biblical world-view," "the Biblical witness," "Biblical theology." Yes; but *which* "world-view" within the Bible; *which* "Biblical witness"? It is a critic of Liberal Theology who finds himself compelled to concede that "one of the most important contributions of liberalism was: . . . . They saw that the Bible contained not one system of pure doctrine from cover to cover. . . . but rather a wide diversity of perspectives which developed over a long period of time. . . . This means that theology must now face squarely the difficult problems having to do with the diversity of thought within the Bible." [25] Precisely. But how are we to tell which Biblical "perspective" is authoritative for Christian Faith? Where lies the norm for the discrimination of truth from error, of the enduring from the transient, of authentic Christian Truth from its imperfect anticipations and its illegitimate elaborations? As we have repeatedly insisted, Liberal Theology locates the decisive norm at one place: the mind and especially the faith of Jesus.

25. Kenneth Cauthen, *The Impact of American Religious Liberalism,* Harper & Row, 1962, p. 217.

The alternative answer to the "new quest" for a locus of Christian truth and authority is: *"the Church."* But, again, *which* Church—the earliest Church of the original Christian community? or the Church at some point or of some period in the nineteen centuries of Christian history, perhaps the Church of the Middle Ages or the Church of the Reformation? [26]

As we shall note in the opening sentences of our appended historical review of "Theology in the Nineteenth Century," [27] contemporary Christians tend to fall victims to "the habit of youth: to disparage their parentage and idealize their remoter ancestry." They "hark back to the 'Founding Fathers' and long for the 'Great Ages' of the past," whether the Age of Reformation or medieval Christendom or the Early Church. The romanticizing tendency which is deep in the religious spirit, which made that spirit such a ready ally of the secular Romantic Movement a century and a half ago, will not down. Today, in one or another school of scholars, it is focussed upon one or another of these three major historic epochs—the Reformation, the Middle Ages, the earliest centuries. The result is that we are being offered, as though reliable historical truth, portraits and interpretations of the Christian Church in each of these eras which are at far remove from that Church as sober and scientific inquiry sets it before us. A survey of current Christian theology might well take as its caption: "Overselling the Church."

For example, Dr. John Knox, searching for the initiating Fact or "Event" which constitutes the earliest and foundational certainty regarding Christianity available to us, proposes the birth of "the early Church" or "the primitive Church." [28]

26. A single illustration of many from which choice might be made is Daniel Jenkins, *The Strangeness of the Church,* Doubleday, 1955.

27. See, below, pp. 155ff.

28. *Op. cit.,* p. 22. I myself find it difficult to reconcile Dr. Knox's latest

What is this "early Church" or "primitive Church" to which appeal is so widely made by today's scholars? We are not without trustworthy and revealing pictures of that earliest Christian community, for example in the Book of Acts and in Paul's letters, especially to the Corinthians. The corporate reality there vividly portrayed is hardly one upon which a Faith for today and for all time could be based. Our respect, even reverence, for those earliest Christians who had been gripped first by the majesty of Jesus himself and then by the power of his living Presence, which steeled them for bold conflict with traditional Judaism and the multifarious paganisms of the Graeco-Roman world of their day even to martyrdom, knows no bounds. But neither their life nor their faith furnish adequate norms or authority for a Christianity which must live in utterly different circumstances, notably our own day.

As to the *life* of that "Primitive Church," some of the most characteristic and vivid features of the Church in Corinth as Paul unveils them in his *First Letter* are:

in the personal lives of the Corinthian Christians: gluttony, drunk-

position with that which informs many of his earlier writings: e.g., *The Man Christ Jesus,* Willett, Clark & Co., 1941; *Christ the Lord,* Willett, Clark, & Co., 1945; *On the Meaning of Christ,* Scribners, 1947; (these three works have been re-published in a single volume, *Jesus, Lord and Christ,* Harpers, 1958), and especially his *The Ethic of Jesus in the Teaching of the Church,* Abingdon, 1961, in which the words of Jesus recorded in the Synoptic Gospels are throughout used as though they were authentic reports of his actual teaching. For example, in the last-named volume, Dr. Knox speaks in his "Foreword" of the teachers within the Early Church "to whom we are no doubt in debt for the blocks of Jesus' own ethical teaching which have been preserved for us" (p. 10); and later develops at great length, as one of the most striking and challenging themes of his book, the contrast between Jesus' teaching on Divine forgiveness and Paul's doctrine of justification by faith (Cht. IV). Yet Paul's influence upon the thought of the Early Church was a powerful if not dominating one. How are we to account for the contrast between Paul's thought on this central issue of Christian Faith and that of the reported words of Jesus except on the assumption that the latter, in such striking contradiction of what Paul and Acts and other New Testament writings teach, were, in fact, reliably remembered and recorded?

enness even at celebrations of the Lord's Supper, gross immorality, infidelity in marriage;

within the fellowship of the Church of Corinth itself: divisions, factionalism, petty jealousy, squabbling;

in the public worship of that Church: idolatry, emotional ecstasies, unrestrained and rather revolting excesses.[29]

Dr. Reinhold Niebuhr, I think it was, who once suggested that the burden of Paul's plea to Christ's followers in Corinth was: "Now that you have become Christians, try to behave as decently as your pagan neighbors." And yet there is no reason to suppose that, in these respects, the Christian community in Corinth was wholly unrepresentative of its sister-Churches of the earliest period.

As to the *Faith* of that initial Church, it was dominated by confidence in an early catastrophic Return of Jesus, a wholly mistaken expectation which was refuted and discredited by the actual course of history.

Moreover, that the earliest Christians gravely misunderstood Jesus and departed radically from his teaching and his own faith stands forth upon the record. The dominant facts are summed up in the mature twofold judgment of the last of the Gospels:

> *"He was in the world, and the world knew him not."*
> *"He came to his own, and his own received him not."*[30]

These tragic but true statements applied not only to the response to Jesus in his lifetime, but hardly less to that of the first Christians. Indeed, one of the most powerful (and neglected) evidences of the authenticity of large segments of the recorded words of Jesus, for example the Sermon on the Mount and the great stories in Luke

29. I Corinthians, 1–12.

30. John 1:10–11.

(Chapters 9–19) is the vivid contrast between this teaching and that of the early Church as it is recorded for us both in Acts and in Paul's letters.

The first of these two declarations of the Fourth Gospel defines Jesus' relation to *Society*—in the first instance, of course, the "world" in which his life was lived, the world which committed him to the Cross; but hardly less, the "world" which his Living Spirit is forever seeking to penetrate and to claim for the principles and purposes of the Living God, his Father. The second and far more poignant and devastating declaration accurately describes Jesus' relation to "his own," in the first instance, his People, Israel, but also his relatives, his immediate followers—here is the supreme pathos of Jesus' life and death; and, hardly less—and this is the focus of our present concern—his continuing followers in the First Century; yes, and even through all the centuries.

We tend to think of the relation of Christ to the World almost altogether in terms of confrontation—Christ's Judgment upon Society and the World's rejection of Christ. We overlook the fact that, from the first moment, the relationship was much more intimate, the influence reciprocal. If Christ is known to us as one who stands over against the World, judging it, one whose rightful role is to permeate and redeem it, it is no less the fact that, from the very first moment of his life, the World not only stood over against Christ in rejection, but also penetrated men's understanding of him and moulded their conception of him to its own desires, its own image.

That moulding, that distortion, began before his birth, in the anticipations of the Christ, in the prevailing conceptions of the Coming Saviour, voiced in the Angel's promise to Mary and Mary's Magnificat: "He hath put down the mighty from their seats and exalted them of low degree."; and in Zacharias' forecasts which we repeat at each Christmastide *as if* they had been fulfilled by Jesus, when, in fact, they were negated by his whole life when they were not explicitly denied by his speech. It is hardly an imaginative exaggeration to picture the infant Jesus, a helpless babe, from the moment of his birth being played upon by men's preconceptions, their yearnings, their expectations, striving to mould him to their desires, falsifying his true Reality.

If we were seeking for a single word to describe the atmosphere of Palestine at the eve of Jesus' birth, it would be: expectation, anticipation, fevered waiting for a Deliverer. To be sure, it took variant forms as it gripped men's imaginations:

Some believed that God would raise up a *human King,* of the lineage of David, to free His People from the rule of Rome by military might. So, Mary understood it.

Some, that God would send an *agent,* a representative, a vice-gerent, "a heavenly Being of human aspect"—half-man, half-God—clothed with the powers of Deity, but appearing in the semblance of Humanity—to establish God's Reign on earth.

Others hoped that *God Himself* would come, in an act of Divine Fiat and deliver His Chosen People from oppression.

The images varied. But all were agreed—deliverance was near; God would effect the deliverance; it would redeem men and reverse the tides of history.[31]

Not only at Jesus' birth, but all through his life, this was the explosive atmosphere, seething with unrest, with passionate hope, charged with fire, in which all his days and works were cast. Into that atmosphere of expectation, Jesus was born.

This anticipation must have been among the most powerful influences playing upon his mind and heart throughout his youth, especially as awareness of his own filial duty to his heavenly Father

31. While there may have been pre-Christian anticipations of a Suffering Messiah in Judaism, these were not dominant. Cf. W. D. Davies, *Paul and Rabbinic Judaism.*

began to form and grow, as an early dim premonition took shape in a deepening consciousness of a special relation to God and special vocation on God's behalf. Is not that the central significance of the "Temptation" episode—the firm rejection of current misguided expectations of that vocation?

Jesus attempted to recast radically, decisively, his contemporaries' ideas of the meaning of deliverance and the manner of its accomplishment. His mind was released from the grip of false expectation. But, he never succeeded in emancipating and redirecting the peoples' anticipations. *The World* was not prepared to receive the *true* Jesus; it "knew him not."

Straight through his life, he had to struggle against misunderstandings and misrepresentations, not only among the populace, but among *his own People:*

> from his mother's misguided hope at his conception;
> and Simeon's faulty jubilation at his birth ("Lord, now let Thy servant depart in peace, for my eyes have seen Thy salvation!");
> through his parents' misunderstanding of him in his youth;
> and, his disciples' repeated efforts to deflect him from his clear and lonely path into the well-worn ruts of the accepted ideas of deliverance ("Get behind me, you Satan, you think the thoughts of men, not of God!").
> right on, through his life to its bitter end—and beyond the end.

The two disheartened followers, making their dejected way to Emmaus on the first Easter afternoon, voiced the general disillusionment: "We *supposed* it had been he who would have delivered Israel." This was the more bitter truth: His own people were unready for him; "He came to his own, and his own received him not."

The whole of his career could be justly interpreted in terms of this single motif; it runs through almost every day and incident of his life: *Men's false expectations of their Saviour* and *Jesus' frustrated failure to bring them into his understanding of salvation, to bring them to receive and accept him as he really was.*

Yes; *but,* we are tempted to say, after his death, especially after his resurrection—all was different! Was it? It was the same World. The same factors continued to play upon both the memories of his life and his Living Presence; and he was no longer present in the flesh, to protest and partially to correct.

We discern the process at work within our Gospels: the heightening of miraculous wonder-working; the inclusion of the very interpretations of himself which he had rejected as mistaken.

If the first Christians so misunderstood and misrepresented the mind of Jesus that neither their life nor their faith can furnish a determinative norm for Christian truth, the same judgment must be made upon the Church of the succeeding centuries. We have already noted the fashion in which the earliest Gospel was penetrated and to some degree perverted by alien influences from the environing culture into which it moved: pagan superstition and magic, concerning Baptism and the Eucharist and the manner and means of God's saving act for mankind; still later, the development of a massive ecclesiasticism and sacerdotalism—to further the cause of One who had derided just such threats to devotion. And we have observed that these distortions found their most striking and their most baneful expression precisely in the attempts to interpret the heart of the Faith, Jesus Christ himself, so that historic Christology was always heretical or semi-heretical.[32]

32. See, above, pp. 29–34, 44–46. Is there clearer evidence that the historic creeds inadequately represent the mind of Jesus than the fact that in the whole of the major creedal affirmations there is not a single reference to the reality which runs as one of the major connecting threads through Jesus' entire teaching, i.e. *the Kingdom of God.* The infrequency of references to the Kingdom in the

It was a process held somewhat in check by the records of his life, a process corrected in part from time-to-time by return to the Gospels' portrait of him, what he really was, his conviction concerning himself and his faith.

As for the Churches of the Reformation, while their aim was to "recover" the aboriginal Faith, their return was to the message of the Primitive Church rather than to Jesus himself; their major textbooks were the Epistles rather than the Gospels. Not until "modern times" was docetism thoroughly excised from Christianity's interpretation of Jesus, and a serious and thorough-going attempt made to take his mind as norm for Christian Faith, i.e. a bold and consistent fidelity to the conviction of the Incarnation, that in the thought of Jesus we find set forth the mind of God, so that his "faith" in his Father constitutes the norm and the essence of authentic Christian Faith. The history of Christian Theology might, not altogether unfairly, be read in terms of a single motif; it runs, like a sad and tragic obbligato, through all the centuries and almost all branches of the Church: *Men's false interpretations of Jesus Christ; Jesus' frustrated failure to bring his followers into understanding of his way and into obedience to his faith.* This is decisive reason why "the Church"—whether the earliest Christian community or the Church through the centuries or at any particular point during those centuries—cannot furnish an adequate and satisfying locus of Christian truth and authority.

In summary, an attempt to ground Christian Faith for our time upon either an undefined and uncriticized "Biblical witness" or upon the life and faith of the Early or the later Church can hardly be made

New Testament after the Synoptic Gospels is, likewise, striking proof both of the authenticity of the reports of Jesus' teaching in the Synoptics and of the sharp contrast between his teaching and the faith of the Early Church.

"intelligible and credible, comprehensible and convincing to intelligent, informed and honest minds of today."

We can only sketch in outline the assumptions regarding our knowledge of Jesus which is essential for Liberal Theology, in my view for *any* authentic Christian Theology.

It is assumed that we possess and shall continue to possess, as the Christian Church has always believed itself to possess, sufficiently clear and reliable knowledge of Jesus to furnish a determinative norm for the continuing reality of Jesus Christ, and thereby for Christian Faith and Life.

It is assumed that the compilers of the Gospels intended, according to the standards of their day, to give faithful representations of Jesus. It is assumed that behind their accounts lie, even if at second or third remove, eyewitnesses' reminiscences. It is assumed that there was continuity, though by no means complete continuity, between the record and its initiating cause, and that on the whole the stream has not risen higher than its source. It is assumed that alteration in transmission has been mainly in the direction of lowering and distorting the original rather than in the direction of heightening and refining it. Thus alterations may to some degree be detected and corrected. In some measure, the records embody their own instrument of correction, just as the Christian Movement through the centuries has contained its own instrument of self-purification. In each instance, the instrument is the same: the impression made by the actual Gospel record upon the most sensitive and sympathetic readers. What we are given, of course, is no photographic reproduction. It cannot be too emphatically insisted that no single sentence or incident need be claimed as indisputably authentic. But, from the whole, there comes forth a portrait, or group of portraits. In the large, these portraits do not cancel one another out. Rather, they both amplify and correct each other to yield a composite portrait of adequate clarity and reliability. The outlook of that person upon the greater issues of life and faith is sufficiently discernible.

An excellent illustration of the application of these presuppositions to a specific facet of Jesus' mind is developed by Dr. John C. Bennett: Jesus' radical attitude toward social exclusiveness and superiority is shown to be attributed to him in the various strands and levels of record with such consistency that its authenticity can hardly be gainsaid.[33]

Another illustration is Jesus' unfailing linkage of religion and life, of faith and morals, of men's relation to God and their relations with each other, of the divine forgiveness and human forgiveness: "Why call ye me 'Lord, Lord' and do not what I say." "Not everyone who says 'Lord, Lord' shall enter into the Kingdom of Heaven, but he who does the Will of my Father in Heaven." "If you forgive not your brother, no more will God forgive you." "If you, though evil, know how to do good to your children, how much more your Father in Heaven."

The supreme illustration is at the pivotal center of faith: Jesus' unfailing use of a single word to identify God, "Father."

Let us recall that the Reality which has served the Christian Movement as determinative norm has not been the scholars' biography of Jesus, or the theologians' construct of Christ. It has been the figure portrayed in the Gospels. In every age, and not least our own, the plain man, picking up this plain tale in his pitiable ignorance of critical principles and theological presuppositions, has found himself gripped by a living man of history who not only stands out upon the records with remarkable clarity but reaches forth from the records to conscript the devotion of his soul.

Textual and historical scholarship—and, more important, the far

33. *Christian Realism,* Scribners, 1941, pp. 126ff.

rarer and more profound skill of historical imagination—may increasingly correct and clarify that portrait. It is unlikely to alter the dominant impression made by the Gospels upon the most sensitively attuned spirits through the centuries, or radically to alter the influence exerted by the picture within the Gospels. Through those admittedly imperfect records, Jesus ever afresh lays constraint upon the Movement which bears his name, holding it more or less true to his intention and faith, and impelling it to new advances for the fulfillment of his purposes in the world. This is the most important fact about the Christian Religion as an historic phenomenon.

We have neither space nor competence to resolve the scholarly issue. We can insist upon its importance. The contemporary paraphrase of Paul's formula of salvation, it has been suggested, might be:

> "By myth are you saved, through symbol; and that not of yourselves; it is the gift of the form-critics."

But, there is no salvation in symbol, far less in myth. For a symbol is, in principle, no more than a signpost, pointing toward Reality. And myth, if not true to its original meaning of fairy-tale, is, at most, a pictorial suggestion of Reality. There is no salvation save in God. And salvation which may rightly be named "Christian" is through Incarnation: through God, the Living God, the One and only True God, in the true man, Jesus of Nazareth and that same Living Person across the Ages and today.

If I may be permitted an autobiographical *confessio,* I was not won from sophomoric indifference or sophisticated scepticism by an exposition of the Faith of the "Primitive Church" or by a proclamation of Christian dogma or by the contemporary Church; almost without a single exception, the impressions made upon me by that Church through boyhood and youth were negative when they were not definitely repellent. As with the two witnesses from China quoted above, I was won by the towering eminence and inescapable truth of the mind and life, the spirit and faith, of Jesus of Nazareth.[34]

My colleague, Dr. James Muilenburg, has recently summarized Jesus' meaning for him as the conclusion of an intimate and informal talk on "What I Believe it Means to be Saved" as follows:

> "Finally and climactically, I know something of what it means to be 'saved', to be liberated and emancipated through Jesus, the Christ of Israel. But this must not become a mere formula or cliche; if it is, it is better left unsaid. Rightly or wrongly, I am conscious of an historical person, of the face that looks at us in the gospels, of one who walked the roads of Palestine, and is still the present companion. I think of Jesus and the prostitutes and tax-gatherers, the undesirables and those who have no one to speak up for them, of Jesus who has stories to tell and is always opening doors, like raising windows to life as it is, who will not follow the patterns of the respectable, but is constantly shattering the conventions and the grooves. *Of course,* I believe in the Incarnation and in Jesus Christ the risen Lord, but I do not think of the *logos* or the Word without the life that was lived among us. If the record in the Gospels is all the fabrication of the early church, then one may ask whether we can in truth speak of an historical revelation. I know that this view is not popular in many quarters today; but here I must take my stand, not because I wish it to be true, but because there seems to me to be substantial evidence that it is true. I think of Jesus, then, as one who reveals the power of God's love—and how powerful that love was! And in so

34. As set forth, for example, in T. R. Glover, *The Jesus of History,* Association Press, 1917; Harry Emerson Fosdick, *The Manhood of the Master,* Association Press, 1918; J. A. Robertson, *The Spiritual Pilgrimage of Jesus,* London, James Clark & Co., 1918; etc. Although they require revision in the light of later studies, they still seem to me to set forth a, on the whole, convincing portrait of the historic Person. Cf. such more recent interpretations of Jesus as Mary Ely Lyman, *Jesus,* Association Press, 1937; J. W. Bowman, *The Intention of Jesus,* Westminster, 1943; Walter Russell Bowie, *I Believe in Jesus Christ,* Abingdon, 1959; and my *Life's Meaning,* Association Press, 1951, Cht. 4.

> doing, he brings to fruition and fulfilment the motif of love that is already present in the hour of the Exodus. I know now that it was love that moved God to enter into man's history, that it was love that moved Him to create the universe, and that it was love that suffered on the Cross."

I would associate myself fully with Dr. Muilenburg's statement, and make it my own.

If the sceptical conclusions of those contemporary scholars who tell us that we cannot really know that Person and that it is not important that we should, should finally prevail, then both intellectual honesty and ethical integrity would compel me not merely to renounce the Christian ministry and resign from membership in the Church, but to surrender adherence to Christian Faith. This is not an extravagant overstatement for dramatic effect; it is sheer statement of fact. I venture to declare it only to illustrate what, for at least one Christian and I suspect for countless others, is at stake in the certitude of Jesus of Nazareth as the source-spring and foundation of Christian Faith.

Christian Faith without the figure of Jesus is like a portrait with an elaborate and impressive frame and a variegated mat but lacking the Face of the subject.

We have already noted the quite extraordinary attention to and acceptance of the interpretation of Jesus Christ by the late Professor Donald M. Baillie of St. Andrews University when it first appeared some fifteen years ago.[35] No treatment of Christology in our lifetime has won so nearly universal acclaim from so many Christian scholars of virtually every point of view and persuasion. Our earlier reference to Dr. Baillie's work focussed upon his definitive (and devastating) judgment that virtually all theological explanations of Jesus Christ

35. D. M. Baillie, *God Was in Christ: An Essay on Incarnation and Atonement*, Scribners, 1948.

across the Christian centuries, especially as they were crystallized in the Creeds, were "continually haunted by a docetism which made His human nature very different from ours and indeed largely explained it away as a matter of simulation or 'seeming' rather than reality" (p. 11); in other words, classical Christology was heretical, or, at best, semi-heretical. (See, above p. 45) We quoted Dr. Baillie's own summary of the historical record: "The cruder forms of docetism were fairly soon left behind, but in its more subtle forms the danger continued in varying degrees to dog the steps of theology right through the ages *until modern times*." (itals. added); and urged that recognition of this fact of history supplies the context in which the new interpretation of Christ which has been set forth "in modern times," e.g. by Liberal Theology, should be viewed and appraised.

I cannot better conclude this consideration of the decisive importance of Jesus for Christian Faith than to invite Dr. Baillie to declare the position which I myself would wish to advance, for my own conviction coincides with his at almost every major point, and I cannot hope to surpass the matchless clarity, balance and persuasion of his presentation of it:

> "The Christian doctrine of the Incarnation does not mean that Jesus was not a man but a God. The New Testament writers knew very well that He was a man, and spoke of Him quite unequivocally as such." (p. 80)
>
> "Does Christianity, then, teach that God changed into a Man? Is that the meaning of 'and was made man'? That at a certain point of time God, or the Son of God, was transformed into a human being for a period of about thirty years? It is hardly necessary to say that the Christian doctrine of the Incarnation means nothing like that." (p. 82)
>
> "We have to reckon with a life that was wholly human and wholly divine, neither side limiting the other at all." (p. 93)

"Jesus was a real man, subject to the conditions and limitations of humanity, with a human will that had to make its continual choices in face of life's temptations, and thus His goodness must be quite realistically regarded as a human achievement." (p. 130)

"It must, of course, be true that His choices were genuine human choices, and that in a sense everything depended upon them." (p. 130)

"Jesus Christ is the One in whom human selfhood fully came to its own and lived its fullest life, as human life ought to be lived, because His human selfhood was wholly yielded to God, so that His whole life was the life of God." (p. 145)

"Jesus lived His life in complete dependence on His Father, as we all ought to live our lives." (p. 93)

"When at last God broke through into human life with full revelation and became incarnate, must we not say that in a sense it was because here at last Man was perfectly receptive? If the life of our Lord is to be conceived as a truly human life, subject to the hazards of all human life on earth, we must indeed say that the Incarnation of the Divine Word in Him was conditioned by His continual response. If it was a real Incarnation, not to be explained away in the docetic manner, it depended in a sense upon His free human choice from moment to moment. . . . It represents the Father's love for the Son as conditional on His fulfilling His vocation." (p. 149)

"Christology stands for a Christian interpretation of history, but it can stand for that only because it stands for the conviction that God became man in the historical person of Jesus. We must have a Christology in that sense, or we have no Christology at all, and we cannot escape from its traditional problems by turning it into a symbolical philosophy of history." (p. 79)

On the essentiality, for a true Christian Faith, of our possessing adequate and trustworthy knowledge of Jesus' life and words and work, Dr. Baillie has this to say:

"There is no stability in a position which accepts to the full the humanity of Christ but has no interest in its actual concrete mani-

> festation and doubts whether it can be recaptured at all; which insists on the 'once-for-allness' of this divine incursion into history, but renounces all desire or claim to know what it was really like. . . . . However defective theologically the 'Jesus of history' movement may have been, however unscientific and over-imaginative its confident reconstructions of the historic portrait, and however one-sided its attempt to make a religion out of such a reconstruction alone, the reaction against it has been equally one-sided and gives up something that we cannot give up if Christianity is a 'historical' religion at all." (p. 28)
>
> "Indispensable, surely, is the actual portrait of the historical Jesus. . . . . Apart from that, we do not know why we should say these things *about a particular historical figure,* Jesus the carpenter of Nazareth. In short, we do not know who it is about whom we say these marvellous things, and therefore cannot know why we say them. . . . . Nor can we justify this on the ground of the witness and authority of the Church; for apart from all authentic knowledge of the personality of the Jesus of history it is difficult to see how the Church itself could continue to be justified in saying these things about a particular historical figure." (p. 52)

Finally, Dr. Baillie comes to the central perplexity for all truly orthodox understanding of Jesus Christ: *how* one who was fully human can also have been truly Divine, God incarnate in the life of Jesus of Nazareth:

> "The real problem for all schools . . . . is: In what sense do we believe that this human life of Jesus of Nazareth was at the same time . . . . the very life of God Himself." (p. 20)

Professor Baillie seeks light on this central mystery of the Faith through an examination of "paradox." Here, he is on ground thoroughly familiar to the mind of today. But he finds in paradox, not an escape from thought, but an illumination of understanding. He stresses the omnipresence of paradox in human life and, more particularly, at "every vital point" in Christian Faith—e.g. when we attempt to understand Creation or Providence. "This is not the only point at which we are beset with paradox in our Christian belief: this is rather the point at which the constant and ubiquitous paradox reaches its peak." (p. 106) In other words, the mystery of the Incarnation is not, in principle, without analogy in other crucial areas of human experience. We gain our most rewarding comprehension of it through an examination of "the paradox of grace."

It is a common-place of all Christian experience that every good thing the Christian does is, at one and the same time, his own act *and* God's act in him. This is the paradox of human freedom and Divine Grace. "This paradox in its fragmentary form in our own Christian lives is a reflection of that perfect union of God and man in the Incarnation." (p. 117) Indeed, the vigorous assertion of the real humanity of Jesus quoted above needs to be completed:

> "Jesus was a real man, subject to the conditions and limitations of humanity, with a human will that had to make its continual choices in face of life's temptations, and thus His goodness must be quite realistically regarded as a human achievement. But goodness in a human life, even in small proportions, is *never* simply a human achievement. . . . All goodness in a human life is wrought by God. That is the other side, and somehow that side comes first, without destroying the human. . . . The divine is always prevenient."
>
> (p. 130)

The point most to be stressed regarding Professor Baillie's interpretation is not simply that the mystery which lies at the heart of Christian Faith is explained in terms of paradox, which is an all too familiar feature of man's experience at all its deepest levels, but that it is explained in terms of a particular paradox, the "Paradox of Grace," which is not peculiar to Christ but characterizes all highest living. Jesus' experience is thus brought into vital analogy to our own experience (which is simply to take his humanity with utmost seriousness), and yet its transcendent supremacy remains unimpaired.

> "If then Christ can be thus regarded as in some sense the prototype of the Christian life, may we not find a feeble analogue of the incarnate life in the experience of those who are His 'many brethren,' and particularly in the central paradox of their experience: 'Not I, but the grace of God'? If this confession is true of the little broken fragments of good that are in our lives—if these must be described on the one hand as human achievements, and yet on the other hand, and in a deeper and prior sense, as *not* human achievements but things actually wrought by God—is it not the same *type* of paradox, taken at the absolute degree, that covers the whole ground of the life of Christ, of which we may say that it was the life of a man and yet also, in a deeper and prior sense, the very life of God incarnate?" (p. 129)

It cannot be contended (and, doubtless, Dr. Baillie would have been the first to disavow any such claim) that this interpretation of Jesus Christ solves the age-old baffling dilemmas of Christology—especially the precise relations between the Divine Initiative and the human initiative (or human response) in the personality of Jesus. But it does place that central dilemma in relation to a parallel dilemma in all highest human experience—the central dilemma, indeed, in our attempts to interpret human personality. This perplexity in understanding the Person of Christ is, *in principle,* no different and no more difficult than the relation of divine initiative and human response in all human action. Here we face the ultimate mystery in every human personality; and in Jesus in supreme degree just because he is the one true human person.[36]

36. For a somewhat fuller summary of Professor Baillie's argument in his *God Was in Christ,* see "A Fresh Interpretation of Christ" in *Christianity and Crisis,* December 25, 1950.

Dr. C. H. Dodd, universally recognized as among the greatest Biblical scholars of our day, who has maintained a sane and sound course through all the swirling and fluctuating currents of New Testament interpretation which have swept so many of his colleagues far off center, concludes his commentary on the First Letter of John with this admonition:

> "The safeguards which this epistle recommends are, to live within the fellowship of the Church, and to adhere loyally and with understanding to the authentic tradition of the Apostles; keeping always in view that which the apostles attest, and which creates the fellowship of the Church—the historical revelation of God in the life and words of Jesus Christ." [37]

Christianity could, if necessary, get along without many things often held to be indispensable for its survival, though not without loss; and has, in fact, done so: without formal church structure, since there was none at the outset; without an ordained ministry—God be praised for the Friends, the Salvation Army and others!; without a creed, beyond the original Apostolic Confession: "Jesus is Lord."

Christianity bereft of the figure and face, the mind and above all the faith of Jesus of Nazareth would doubtless continue as an important religious movement in the world. In due time, it would no longer be identifiable as authentic Christian Faith. It would be discovered to have lost Christianity's *sine qua non,* the secret of its power in the world: of its continuity and inner cohesion, which lie, not in ecclesiastical tradition or organization or declaration, but in the binding power of that Figure; its authority which speaks, not through men's formularies, but through the Voice of God in the voice of Jesus Christ; its unique capacity for self-criticism and renewal; its power for expansion and extension, rekindled ever and again across the centuries through fresh contact with that Person.

37. C. H. Dodd, *The Johannine Epistles,* Harper, 1946, p. 142.

Nothing less than this is at stake in the Church's certitude of its central reality, its fulcrum, its animating heart—Jesus Christ, disclosed in power in the Living Christ of the centuries, but defined as to authenticity in the life and mind and faith of Jesus of Nazareth.

2. We come next to our second question: Can the Christian affirmation concerning Jesus Christ—that he was truly a man, yet also God uniquely present in human life—be made intelligible to the mind of today?

A first principle is *resolute and rigorous adherence to appropriate and adequate terminology*. The vocabulary of interpretation should be drawn unfailingly from living and familiar words of ordinary human speech rather than from the abstract and largely sterile categories of traditional physics and metaphysics. Jesus Christ should be described, whether in his relations to God or to man, not in such terms as "substance," "essence," "infinity," "immutability," "impassability," but always in words descriptive of personal life such as "thought," "will," "purpose," "self," "spirit," "goodness," "love." This principle is to be insisted upon not as a concession to simplification. Rather it is dictated by the fact that the Reality with which we have to deal is, in its every aspect, intrinsically and richly personal—as a human person, living a normal and normative human experience; as a powerful personal influence in history; as a living personal Presence today. Adequately to account for that Reality, no terms should be employed drawn from another and lower level than that of personal spiritual life. When it is recalled that traditional Christologies took their vocabularies largely from what to us are lower levels of reality than that of personal, spiritual experience, their inadequacy is apparent. They are suspect primarily, not because they are overstatements of the facts, but because they may be understatements and so false-statements.

Firmly resolved upon the use of appropriate terms only, how shall the interpretation proceed? The problem for the mind of today is, as it has always been, a dual one. It concerns the relation of God to Jesus of Nazareth *and* the relation of Jesus Christ to other men. It breaks into these two related questions:—

1). In what if any sense can God be said to become incarnate in normal or normative human nature, a true human life?

2). In what if any sense can there be said to have taken place a definitive Incarnation of God in Jesus Christ?

For both questions the basic issue is that of "continuity" vs. "radical discontinuity." As we confronted it in the preceding chapter, this is the central issue in almost every theological controversy: whether continuity or radical discontinuity most accurately defines the relations of the world and God, of "Nature" and man, of man and God, of nature and grace; of men's knowledge of Nature and their knowledge of God, of natural and revealed religion; of ethics and religion; of general culture and religion, of non-Christian religions and Christianity; of unredeemed and redeemed human nature; of prophets and saints and Jesus Christ; of Jesus of Nazareth and the Risen Christ, of the faith of Jesus and the faith of the Church, of Christ and the Movement which bears his name. For all religion, the issue comes to clearest focus in the problem of incarnation—whether continuity or discontinuity most accurately defines the relations of God and man. For Christian Faith, the issue comes to decisive focus in the Incarnation of Jesus Christ—the affirmation that in him God was uniquely present. In this perspective, the two questions may be restated:

1). Is the relation of God to man of such a kind that incarnation of God in a human life can be affirmed only through radical miracle, that is through a divine act without anticipation or analogy in God's other relations with His world?

2). Is the relation of Jesus Christ to prophets and saints of such a kind that the Incarnation can be affirmed only through radical miracle, that is through a divine act without anticipation or analogy in God's relations with other men?

1). An answer to the general problem of incarnation must precede any attempt to wrestle with Christian Faith's affirmation concerning the Incarnation of God in Jesus Christ. If radical discontinuity characterizes the normal relations of God and man, there can have taken place no Incarnation as Christian Faith affirms it; for that Incarnation is held to have occurred in a *truly human* person. Unless God is in some measure incarnate in the life of every man, He cannot have become fully incarnate in Jesus of Nazareth. As Dean Matthews declares: "The two pivotal dogmas of developed Christianity are that man is made in the image of God and that God is made manifest fully in the man Christ Jesus." [38] If the two convictions are not interdependent, at least the second cannot stand without the first. So concerned was William Temple to establish this point that, midstream in his great Gifford Lectures, he introduced an entire paragraph in italics. This paragraph may be regarded as the fulcrum of his argument. Indeed, the importance which he attached to it is indicated by the fact that it is reproduced in full in his essay in the symposium on *Revelation.*

"We affirm, then, that unless all existence is a medium of Revelation, no particular Revelation is possible; for the possibility of Revelation depends on the personal quality of that supreme and ultimate Reality which is God. If there is no ultimate Reality, which

38. W. R. Matthews, *God in Christian Experience,* Harpers, 1930, p. 39.

is the ground of all else, then there is no God to be revealed; if that Reality is not personal, there can be no special revelation, but only uniform procedure; if there be an ultimate Reality, and this is personal, then all existence is revelation. Either all occurrences are in some degree revelation of God, or else there is no such revelation at all; for the conditions of the possibility of any revelation require that there should be nothing which is not revelation. Only if God is revealed in the rising of the sun in the sky can He be revealed in the rising of a son of man from the dead; only if He is revealed in the history of Syrians and Philistines can He be revealed in the history of Israel (Amos ix. 7); only if He choses all men for His own can He choose any at all; only if nothing is profane can anything be sacred. It is necessary to stress with all possible emphasis this universal quality of revelation in general before going on to discuss the various modes of particular revelation; for the latter, if detached from the former, loses its root in the rational coherence of the world and consequently becomes itself a superstition and a fruitful source of superstitions. But if all existence is a revelation of God, as it must be if He is the ground of its existence, and if the God thus revealed is personal, then there is more ground in reason for expecting particular revelations than for denying them." [39]

But is the idea of incarnation of God in a human life credible? Here, the matter of terminology becomes crucial. If God be thought of in abstract metaphysical categories—infinity, immutability, impassibility, substance, essence—incarnation is impossible. This, of course, was the fatal weakness of the ancient Christologies. So sympathetic an interpreter as Canon Raven describes the predicament of Christian theologians in the creedal period thus:

"If once God and man are regarded as by postulate irreconcilable . . . all belief in incarnation breaks down. Regarding God as unknowable, impassible, superessential, a dilemma confronted them: either the Logos like ourselves is passible, in which case *ex hypothesi*

39. *Nature, Man and God,* Macmillan & Co. Ltd and St. Martin's Press, 1934, pp. 306–07.

He cannot be divine; or He is impassible and therefore not man at all; in either case there is no incarnation . . . In the end the Church accepted a middle course which is in reality no solution at all . . . Starting from its postulates no other result was possible. Its postulates were unchristian." [40]

On the other hand, if God be thought of as intelligent, holy, purposeful Personality, He may become incarnate within the persons of men. Indeed, strictly speaking, God can indwell *only* intelligent purposeful persons. This is the highest if not the only proper meaning of the immanence of God, incarnation. Immanence is the presence in human spirits of some measure of the Divine Vision and Purity and Purpose, that is of the Divine Life. Complete immanence would occur in a genuine human person who shared, as fully as is possible for a truly human life, the Vision and Purity and Purpose of God. That would be *the* Incarnation.

Precisely this is what Christian Faith affirms to have been true of Jesus Christ. The pith of its contention may be very simply put: *In Jesus of Nazareth, God Himself was present, as fully present as it is possible for Him to be present in a truly human life.* The identity of Jesus with God was of "outlook," of purpose, of will, of action, of compassion.

"We may think of two wills or minds as identical in content while remaining formally distinct . . . Christ was one with the Father in character, in purpose, in love. It is doubtful whether the union of the Son with the Father can be expressed in higher terms than in terms of harmony of mind and spirit, identity of conscious purpose, complete mutual understanding and fellowship and cooperation, community of values . . . To call this unity 'merely ethical' is to fail to appreciate the centrality and ultimacy of ethical values in a Christian philosophy of the universe. The ethical *is* the metaphysical in its most revealing aspect. When we assert that Christ is one with

40. *Apollinarianism,* pp. 37–38.

the Father in character and purpose, we have reached a point beyond which we cannot advance except by a leap into the abyss of an abstract and unknowable Absolute."[41]

Or, in Temple's briefer assertion:

> "The Form of His consciousness is human, its content Divine. The whole content of His Being—His thought, feeling and purpose—is also that of God. That is the only 'substance' of a spiritual being, for it is all there is of him at all."[42]

In summary, in and through Jesus' words and acts and attitudes and inmost spirit, the Life of God spoke and acted as fully as the Sovereign of Reality could find expression through a man of Nazareth in the days of the Caesars. His life was the full meeting-point of divinity and humanity—an individual soul altogether responsive to and possessed by the Divine Intention for him; God indwelling that soul as fully as is possible in a genuine human life. That is the meaning of "a perfect human life," the meaning of "the Divinity of Christ"—the only possible meaning for a Faith resolved to cleave to Christianity's central certainty that Jesus was truly a man, yet also uniquely God in human flesh. The Divinity of Christ affirms that God was as fully present in Jesus of Nazareth as it is possible for Him to be in a truly human person.

2). If the relation of Jesus to God be thus understood, does not Jesus thereby become so removed from ordinary men as to be no longer of mankind? If his divinity be so affirmed, is his humanity credible? This is the second major problem of interpretation.

Here is one place where recent thought has enriched our equipment with a new concept and new categories of promising fruitfulness. If

41. D. Miall Edwards, "A Christology in Modern Terms," in *The Lord of Life,* Macmillan, 1929, pp. 212ff.

42. William Temple in *Foundations,* Macmillan, 1913, p. 248.

valid and relevant, they may offer the possibility of a solution where solution was never previously possible. This is the "doctrine of levels" or philosophy of Emergent Evolution of which we gave a detailed exposition in the earlier discussion of continuity vs. discontinuity.[43]

The doctrine of levels leads us to expect a progressive self-disclosure of the Divine in the ascending strata of reality. Moreover, the "nisus" or drive within the cosmos which is manifest in the emergence of progressively delicate and significant types of reality points beyond its highest realization within our usual apprehension (that is, the loftiest range of normal human achievement, often designated "spirit") toward a still fuller realization of the Divine (often termed "deity"). Furthermore, the empirical facts of the evolutionary process enable us to define what would be the character of that higher level, if and when it should appear. It would occur in a human life in which "spirit" (i.e. recognition of and devotion to ultimate values) was no longer partially dominant but completely regnant. To say the same thing otherwise, it would occur in a human life no longer partly but completely receptive to the Divine Intention and Persuasion; therefore, a life whose thoughts, feelings and purposes were identical with those of the Divine Spirit for him. Such a life would be the full meeting-point of the divine and the human as we have defined it above: a human soul altogether responsive to and possessed by the Divine Purpose for him; God indwelling that soul as fully as is possible in a genuine human life. In summary, the *a priori* specifications for the realization of "deity" developed from a general philosophy of reality precisely correspond to Christian Faith's affirmation concerning the empirical fact of Jesus Christ—one who is at once truly a man and yet also God incarnate.[44]

43. See, above, pp. 83–89.

44. Even so naturalistic a scientist as Lloyd Morgan hazards the suggestion: "If an impartial historical survey should lead to the conclusion that the nisus

"The idea of evolution helps us to find a place for the Jesus of history within the setting of the whole evolutionary scheme, teleologically understood, i.e. to interpret Him as the emergence of a new quality in history without breach of continuity, a natural-supernatural Person, a miracle in accordance with law, as every new quality may be said to be, relatively to that which lies beneath it in the process of 'emergent evolution.'"[45]

3. Lastly, how, more precisely does this personal reality, Jesus Christ, whose power is disclosed in its ever-effective influence upon the life of mankind and whose authenticity is defined by the historic life, furnish determinative norms for authentic Christian Faith? *What is the character and extent of Jesus' authority for our thought and life today?*

Let us recall once again the precise terms of the affirmation concerning Jesus which Christian Faith is constrained to make. It is: *In Jesus of Nazareth, God Himself was as fully present as it is possible for Him to be present in a human life.* Jesus' thought, feeling, will were identical with God's Intention for him. In and through Jesus' words and acts and attitudes and inmost spirit, the Life of God spoke and acted as fully as it was possible for the Sovereign of Reality to find expression through a man of Nazareth in the days of the Caesars. His life was the full meeting-point of divinity and humanity—an individual soul altogether responsive to and possessed by the Divine Intention for him—God indwelling that soul as fully as is possible in a genuine human life. That is the meaning of "a

towards deity has culminated in one unique individual, there is, so far as I can see, nothing in the naturalistic interpretation of emergent evolution which precludes the acceptance of this conclusion." (C. Lloyd Morgan, *Emergent Evolution,* Holt, 1926, p. 31.)

45. D. Miall Edwards, *op. cit.*

perfect human life," the meaning of "the divinity of Christ"—the only possible meaning for a Faith resolved to adhere strictly to Christianity's certainty concerning Jesus, that he was truly a man, yet also uniquely God in human flesh.

More specifically, if a distinction be recognized between those aspects of human experience which are so colored and determined by the special circumstances of time and career as to mark each man from his fellows *and* those aspects of experience which are so persistent, so universal as to recur within every normal human pilgrimage, we may affirm that Jesus' insight into the peculiar problems of his own day and his way of meeting and moulding those problems were the best possible for one of his age, background and experiences, while his insights into those aspects of man's lot which are essentially the same in every age because they are of the fabric of universal humanity and his way of meeting and moulding those perennial issues of human life were true for all men in all times.

This is a very great claim. But it is a claim implying definite limitations. Limitations of knowledge—such knowledge as could normally have been available to a man of Jesus' time, place and circumstance. Limitations of outlook—such breadth of comprehension and depth of insight as could occur in a genuine human spirit of that day. Limitations of divine indwelling, of incarnation. It is a mistake to claim that in Jesus, the whole Being of God was present, that God's Purpose was fully expressed through him. If we are to make earnest with the assertion of Jesus' humanity, we must recognize that only so much of the Being and Purpose of God found expression in and through him as was appropriate and possible for one of his heritage, his era, his span of experience.

Such a view suggests at once the first and principal fashion by which that Presence of God within the person of Jesus may find and guide and aid each of us in the distinctive problems of our age and life. It has been well stated by Canon Hodgson:

> "It is in the Gospels that we find set forth the mind of Christ. It is as we see him in the circumstances of his time, thinking and speaking about the people he met and the things he saw, reflecting on all his experiences of life and showing by his words and deeds how they struck his mind, that we come to know the mind of Christ which is the mind of God. As we come to know it we come to share it, and as we come to share it we come to read aright the very different problems of our own lives and times, and to recognize anew the one eternal goodness in new varieties of its infinite manifestations." [46]

Jesus offers no blueprint for life, an example to be slavishly copied. He offers an illustration of a life lived wholly in fidelity to the Divine Purpose which may instruct and inspire others to bring their quite different lives into conformity with the Divine Will's quite different purposes for them. He serves men, primarily, not as a reservoir from which specific directives may be tapped, but rather as a tuning-fork by which their souls may be attuned to the Divine Spirit, so that that living, ever-present, ever-urgent Spirit may play forth the melodies of their own minds and hearts, their lives and careers in harmony with his Design for them.

Strictly speaking, that is the only fashion in which Jesus (according to the terms of Christian Faith's understanding of him) serves the individual Christian as *absolute* moral authority. The only absolute which a sound Christian ethic recognizes is—God's personal design for each individual human person in every particular circumstance of his life, a design which is a function of God's larger Design for all Mankind. That Design, in its specific incidence, alters from day to day and moment to moment as the total complex of the human situation changes. No discrete moral precept or principle wields abso-

46. Leonard Hodgson, *And Was Made Man,* Longmans, 1928, p. 28.

lute authority save as it is interpreted, becomes concrete, within that larger context of God's living Purpose for all humanity in the here and now. The constancy of God's Purpose is one not of immutability but of intrinsic consistency.

Is there, then, no instrument or device more precisely to define what is essential within the reality of Jesus Christ; for example, what is permanently authoritative in the specific content of Jesus' teaching? There is an instrument which, while not absolutely determinative, is exceedingly fruitful for the more precise demarcation of our norm. There is available for our quest the great, broad deep stream of life and thought which took its rise in Jesus of Nazareth and the tiny band which gathered to his call and who, under compulsion of his continuing Presence, carried their Faith to the world; a stream which has flowed down through nineteen centuries. This is the Christian Movement in the world. That stream has suffered shallows and whirlpools, eddies and stagnant marshes. But there is discernible—indeed, inescapable—*a central current* of both thought and life—clear, strong, relatively pure—which has furnished both direction and power. This central current issued unmistakably from the fountain-source in the mind and practice of Jesus. It has reappeared, issuing afresh and with renewed purity and sweep, from almost every one of the towering figures along the way—Paul and the Johannine writer and James, Origen and Augustine, Bernard and Francis, Aquinas and Erasmus, Luther and Fox and Edwards, Wesley and Newman—down to our own day, what Professor Brightman once called: "the life stream of history under the influence of Jesus." Here is the locus of those elements in the reality of Jesus Christ which have vindicated themselves through the centuries as most indisputably authoritative.

Are we, then, proposing the familiar norm—"quod ubique, quod semper, quod ab omnibus creditum est"? Yes, with the important addition of one word "ab omnibus *sanctis*." And the emphasis falls less upon what has been explicitly affirmed than upon what has been assumed, trusted and practiced.

To be sure, no two persons will survey that main current identically. No two descriptions of the common Faith will wholly coincide. There is the true role of private judgment. And also the safeguard against final crystallization and hard dogmatism. Here is no basis for precise creedal formulation, no measuring-rod for heresy-trials and excummunications. Membership within the Christian Movement is constituted by kinship of effectual faith with the faith of the saints. This would appear to be implicit in the central and regnant certainty on which all Christians are united—the reality of the Incarnation. If Christianity springs from and rests upon a personal life in whom God dwelt, then it is in personal lives continuing in some measure the Incarnation that authentic Christian Faith must be discovered—and there only. Essential Christian Faith is that which has dwelt at the core of the beings of the Great Followers and has linked them in patent continuity with their Lord. And the norm of its authenticity is—unmistakable congruity with the Mind of Christ.

Archbishop William Temple has said much the same thing, in commenting upon the affirmations regarding Christ as the Light of the World in the Fourth Gospel:

> "As we look forward, we peer into darkness, and none can say with certainty what course the true progress of the future should follow. But as we look back, the truth is marked by beacon-lights, which are the lives of saints and pioneers; and these in their turn are not originators of light, but rather reflectors which give light to us because themselves they are turned towards the source of light." [47]

To return to the query, how does the reality of Jesus Christ serve Christian Faith as a determinative norm?

First of all, it determines that which is essential. There is nothing

47. William Temple, *Readings in St. John's Gospel,* Macmillan & Co. Ltd and St. Martin's Press, 1939, Volume I, p. 8.

which is *essential* in Christian belief—nothing—which is not congruous with, indeed implicit in, the recorded faith of Jesus of Nazareth. (This is not the equivalent of the claim that there is nothing in Jesus' belief which is not essential for Christian Faith.) Anything else may be useful and true. It is secondary and accessory. And it is suspect until its intrinsic kinship with the mind of Christ has been demonstrated.

Again, the faith of Jesus is normative for the specific *beliefs of Christian Faith,* for the content of Christian doctrine. The authentic *Christian view of man* makes its beginning, not in the anthropology of Augustine, or of Paul, or of contemporary psychology, but in the largely unuttered yet discernible assumptions of Jesus' outlook disclosed in his conversations with individual men and women. It is doubtful whether a Christian doctrine of man in these terms has often, if ever, been fully worked out. It may be questioned whether such a doctrine would readily find place for the traditional idea of original sin, certainly not for the concepts of total depravity, strict determinism, absolute foreordination. Similarly, with the *Christian idea of God;* strictly, it employs as normative for the conception of the Divine no categories other than, certainly none lower than, the single unfailing designation of Jesus: "Father." Alternatives—those familiar in the history of doctrine or those widely offered today—are suspect because, under careful examination, they are seen to be not an advance upon but a descent from that concept; Christian theism is committed to frank, though critical, anthropomorphism. Likewise, the Christian *interpretation of Christ* himself need not go beyond Jesus' own declarations of his nature and his vocation; more or other than these forever threaten distortion of his true Reality (overstatement falsifies truth no less than understatement), and thus unintentional betrayal of his meaning for men. The first question, and the last, to be put to Christological theories, whether traditional or modern, should be:—Are they consistent with, indeed suggested by, the impression of his own self-consciousness given by the words and deeds of Jesus? Again, the *Movement* which advances his mission in the world and the *Institution* which bears his name before men find their regulatory norm, not in their own theories of their reality, but in the only concept which commanded Jesus' absolute loyalty—the *Kingdom of God*. Here, it will be agreed, is a searching, purging, asceptic test.

If it be suspected that this view smacks of heresy, the rejoinder may be permitted that it hews to the most unimpeachable orthodoxy. It takes with full seriousness the Church's assertion of Incarnation—that God was present in Jesus of Nazareth, disclosing Himself and His Mind with regard to the world and men; and that He continues to speak and to work in accents and actions organically continuous with this normative self-disclosure.

The Church has seldom been fully faithful to its only true norm. As we have repeatedly urged, it was the genius of Liberal Theology that it *was* a return, for both its thought and its life, to Jesus Christ; and that this was the secret of its unparalleled enterprises for the emancipation and transformation of human life.

In any event, this is the secret of Christianity's power in the world—of its continuity, of its authority, of its unique capacity for endless self-renewal. All down the nineteen centuries, as we have said earlier, the portrait of Jesus embedded in the Gospels has worked its ever-repeated transformation—exposing absurdities, chastening excesses, sifting truth from fancy and reality from magic, purifying crude and false notions, rectifying sincere but misguided misinterpretations of himself, stirring imagination, quickening faith, chastening infidelity, winning a devotion ever more intelligent and unalterable. Through those imperfect records, Jesus ever afresh lays constraint upon his Movement in the world, holding it more or less true to his mind and faith, and impelling it to new advances for fulfillment of his purposes. This is the most important single fact about the Christian religion.

CHAPTER FIVE

CONCLUSION

CHAPTER FIVE

CONCLUSION

Fidelity to Truth; Affirmation of Continuity in God's World; Moral and Social Responsibility; The Centrality of Jesus Christ: These are the basic and regnant principles of Liberal Theology, yesterday and today and tomorrow. But, above all and finally: The Truth and Authority of the Life of God in the life of Jesus of Nazareth.

The issue may be put vividly in a quite simple illustration. Some years ago, a group of then "Younger Theologians" were discussing precisely this issue. One of them, at that time strongly under the sway of Karl Barth and a neo-orthodox perspective, justifying insistence upon the transcendent and ineffable majesty and mystery of God, protested: "But the Christian thought of God has always had mystery at its center!" One of his companions replied: "No, Christian thought of God has always had mystery at its periphery. But at its center, the face of Jesus Christ." In the contrast of those two statements lies the decisive issue for Christian Faith always, and more specifically, for our own faith. Here is the heart of Liberal Theology's affirmation:

"God, who commanded light to shine out of darkness (i.e. God the Father Almighty, Maker of Heaven and earth), has shined within our hearts to give the light of the knowledge of the glory of God in the face of Jesus Christ." [1] Here is the crux of Christianity.

1. II Corinthians 4:6.

THE FARTHER BACKGROUND

Theology in the Nineteenth Century

THE FARTHER BACKGROUND:

Theology in the Nineteenth Century[1]

It is often the habit of youth, certainly in our time, to disparage their parentage and idealize their remoter ancestry. Distance tends to lift great figures and events above their common-place surroundings and to enfold them in a roseate aura which magnifies their proportions and disguises their limitations. We hark back to the "Founding Fathers." We long for the "Great Ages" of the past.

In a movement so deeply steeped in history as Christianity, this inveterate human tendency is at its strongest. Christians habitually glory in the achievements of the first centuries, the magnificence of medieval Christendom, the triumphs of the age of Reformation, and judge the Church of today and yesterday a poor thing by comparison. In our day, this nostalgia of the backward-look is greatly aggravated by two contradictory factors—pride in the Modern Age which fosters condescension toward its immediate predecessor and disillusionment over the present scene which encourages glorification of the remoter past. For a half century and more, an assumption has been so widespread within intellectual circles as to be regarded as almost axiomatic: that Christianity both as a faith and as a force in the world stands in extremity, struggling in desperate and losing defense

1. Based upon the "Nineteenth Century and Today" in *The Vitality of the Christian Tradition,* ed. by George F. Thomas (copyright, 1944 by Harper & Brothers) and *The Plain Man Seeks for God,* Cht. Two, (copyright, 1933 by Charles Scribner's Sons).

against a dominant world-view opposed to it and battling against the disintegrating effects of catastrophic world-convulsion.

An assumption so generally held cannot be without a measure of justification. Nevertheless, dispassionate appraisal of facts does not sustain it. From the point of view of practical vitality—energy for geographic extension and power for transformation of culture—the period which lies immediately behind our own and of which we are heirs must be put down as the "Great Century" [2] in the history of Christianity. For the first time, emissaries of the Christian message carried it to the ends of the earth, penetrating every continent and touching almost every people. Interpreters of that message made bold to stake its claim over every aspect of human life, corporate no less than individual. From the point of view of intellectual vigor, the bolder schools of Christian thought drank deep of the intoxicating elixirs of their age—the historical and scientific movements, awareness of a World Culture coterminous with the globe, enthusiasm for social reform, confidence in progress. They rediscovered neglected treasures within the Christian tradition, rephrased its essential tenets in the new universe of discourse, and furnished the Church with an apologetic adequate to sustain its prodigious labors of expansion and permeation.

II

The Visitor from Mars who had chanced upon this planet at the dawn of the nineteenth century would hardly have entertained good hope for the future of Christianity. For more than a century previous, in both faith and life the Christian Church had suffered deepening strain, sterility and loss. In area after area of the world to which Christian missionaries had ventured in the preceding era of vitality and extension, their fragile young churches sickened and died. In Japan, Christianity was driven wholly

2. The phrase is Professor K. S. Latourette's and has become current through its employment in his monumental *A History of the Expansion of Christianity*. See, also, my *World Christianity: Yesterday, Today, and Tomorrow*, and *One Great Ground of Hope: Christian Missions and Christian Unity*.

underground. In China and Korea, persecution harassed the weakling Christian communities. In Latin America, the continent of most notable Christian extension in the previous epoch, adventurers who had sought to subdue a continent under the joint aegis of sword and cross had dissipated their vitalities through lust and greed, and had brought corruption and disrepute upon a Church allied with their conquests. Here and there, along the littoral of Africa, in India and Ceylon, at a few centers in East Asia and Indo-China, on certain islands of the Pacific, tiny Christian outstations could be discovered. Australia, New Zealand and many of the lands of Oceania as yet knew nothing of Western culture and religion. Only rarely, as in the Philippines and Northern Celebes, had Christianity succeeded in winning any considerable proportion of the native populace and in establishing itself as the authentic religion of non-European peoples. More characteristically, the Christian outstations were spiritual adjuncts to the outposts of European political or economic imperialism. Christianity was still quite definitely a Western faith. Its fate as a world religion appeared linked to the future of European conquest. But its continuance even as the faith of Europeans seemed gravely insecure.

Throughout Europe, the only continent where Christianity had succeeded in establishing itself as the dominant religion and where it had flourished with seemingly growing power for ten centuries, the Church was speedily losing its hold upon the common people; its claim to the convinced allegiance of the educated and worldly-wise appeared already gone. In England and Germany, Rationalism, the dominant intellectual vogue, had effected an uneasy liaison with Christian Faith to yield a thin and sterile Deism. In Roman Catholic lands such as France, Rationalism was frankly agnostic or atheistic. Romanticism, the other great enthusiasm of the Age, summoned its devotees to a new religion of Nature, of feeling, of the spirit, but was hardly less disdainful toward the Christian tradition. Voltaire, Rousseau, Diderot; Hobbes, Hume, Bentham; Spinoza; Herder, Goethe, Kant—these were the great prophets of the mind. None of them acknowledged more than lip-service to the traditional Faith. Meantime, the ardor of the masses centered in revolutionary movements which sprang from secular presuppositions and, prophetic of the great revolutionary leader of the nineteenth century, dismissed religion as an opiate of the people. This was patently true of the French Revolution, hardly less of Napoleon and the hopes which rallied to his cause.

Moreover, the forces which had undermined Christianity's influence over great thinkers and popular leaders were working their corrosive effect upon leadership within the churches. The result was sterility and even corruption in their worship and practice. John Buchan thus describes the state of religion in Scotland toward the end of the eighteenth century:

> "Nor was there any compensating vigour of life in that church which had once been the chief voice of Scotland. . . . The dominant party, the Moderates, made religion a thing of social decency and private virtues, and their sober, if shallow, creed was undoubtedly a stabilizing factor in a difficult time. . . . The High-flyers, the other party, were equally void of inspiration, and disputed chiefly on questions of church government. . . . The ministers satirized by Burns in his 'Holy Fair' were representative types, but little overdrawn, of the then church in Scotland—a church from which most that was vital in the national life was deeply estranged." [3]

The English parallels were even more disquieting:—

> "A sodden coarseness characterized what called itself the best society. . . . At the opposite social extreme was the great mass of ignorant, restless, half-brutalized population. . . . Drunkenness was almost universal. . . . Every sixth house in London was a gin shop. . . . After nightfall, London was at the mercy of footpads and desperadoes. . . . The laws were savage but ineffectual. . . . The prisons were sinks of filth, stench, and disease. . . . The test of excellence in religion as well as in politics, art, literature, was reason, moderation, good sense. . . . It is said that the two texts on which most sermons were preached were 'Let your moderation be known to all men', and 'Be not righteous overmuch'." [4]

3. *Sir Walter Scott,* Coward, McCann, 1932, p. 15.

4. C. T. Winchester, *The Life of John Wesley,* Macmillan, 1912, pp. 71–79.

Nor were these conditions confined to Christianity in Europe. Many Americans of today entertain a quite false impression of the influence of the Christian Church at the birth and childhood of the new nation. True, this continent had been settled largely by men and women of profound religious faith. But over large areas, the initial impulse had run thin. The liveliest minds had fallen captive to new modes of thought flowing freely across the Atlantic, especially from France. The period of the Revolution and the Constitution was not notable as an age of faith. A famous item records that in Yale College in one of the early years of the nineteenth century, not a single student could be discovered who would confess himself a Christian. But Yale was probably not more pagan than other seats of learning. Meantime, beyond the scattered white settlements fringing the Atlantic seaboard stretched a vast Indian population virtually untouched, and in their midst dwelt a rapidly propagating Negro race still largely heathen.

Such were the condition and prospect of Christianity at the close of the Napoleonic Wars. These facts could hardly have failed to paint the main outlines of the picture for the Man from Mars. It is by no means so sure that his attention would have been caught by certain other features well-nigh hidden beneath the prevailing currents of proud but cynical intellectualism, of romantic confidence in man and his future, of revolutionary utopianism, of religious indifference and unbelief. It is unlikely that they would have been pointed out to him by whatever humans might have proffered their services to him as guides and interpreters of the times. He might have traversed the length of Germany and heard no mention of a numerically small and culturally inconspicuous sect known as Moravians. To be sure, in England John Wesley had stirred to revival thousands among the underprivileged but few among the moulders of thought or leaders of public life. As for other isolated events—the launching of a number of missionary bodies in England, the founding of the Netherlands Missionary Society in Holland, a gathering of five zealous American undergraduates beneath a haystack at Williamstown—few knew of these events, fewer still would have estimated them as more than inconsequential gestures against the rising tides of secularism. Yet in fact, these modest and unnoted beginnings were to wield a larger determination upon the fate of Christianity in the nineteenth century than the speculations of scholars or the swirling currents of revolution.

III

At the outbreak of the next great international conflict a century later, Christianity had become the professed faith of the Western Hemisphere, both North and South America. In the Pacific basin, Australia, New Zealand and many of the lesser islands harbored predominantly Christian populations. In Africa, Christian influence had worked inland from the seacoasts to establish sizeable and vigorous churches with their educational, medical and other institutions among many native tribes. At least some beginnings of a deeply rooted indigenous church were to be found in every country on the face of the earth excepting Nepal, Afghanistan and Tibet to which alone Christian representatives were still forbidden entrance. Perhaps most noteworthy of all, among the most advanced peoples of the East, those most deeply rooted in ancient Oriental cultures—India, China, Japan—the Christian Movement, though counting in its membership an insignificant minority of their populations was now flourishing under the ever-stronger leadership of native Christians whose influence upon national thought and life was out of all proportion to their numbers. Christianity itself was generally recognized as a formative factor of first importance for the physical, intellectual, social and spiritual progress of these lands. Thus emerged the promise of a Christian faith which should be truly universal and the possibility of a Christian Movement truly ecumenical, representative of all humanity.

These are the most obvious surface facts concerning Christianity in the nineteenth century. By any reasonable test which might be proposed—conversions, growth in membership, adventure into new areas, launching of new enterprises, founding of new societies—it was the period of Christianity's largest vitality and greatest advance in the nineteen centuries.

To recount signs of vigor and growth within the Christian Movement itself, however, is to note hardly half the story. This was also a period of Christianity's largest influence upon the culture of which it formed a part. The nineteenth century was preeminently the century of social advance. It was marked by the greatest succession of crusades for the amelioration and improvement of mankind's life which history records. Beginning with agitation for the ending of the slave trade early in the century, the consciences of men, especially in English-speaking lands, were claimed for one cause after another for human betterment. Prison reform, abolition of chattel slavery, improved factory conditions, the founding of the Red Cross, elimination of child labor, equality for women, universal education, temperance, recognition of organized labor, public health, care of the insane and the infirm, social services, agitation for world peace—these are only the more notable instances in the long list. It cannot be said that Christianity alone was responsible for most of them. But it must be recognized that men and women driven by Christian faith to sacrificial and often heroic exertion in their behalf were vital factors in each. In all but one (the rise of organized labor), Christian leadership appears to have had a determinative influence. John Howard, Florence Nightingale, the Earl of Shaftesbury, David Livingstone, Wilberforce, William Lloyd Garrison, Wendell Phillips, Lincoln, Keir Hardy and the pioneers of the British Labor Movement, Washington Gladden, Walter Rauschenbusch—the roll might be lengthened indefinitely.

How are we to account for this unforeseen and epochal record of extension and penetration by Christianity? The answer is to be found in the marriage of certain features which were born of the times and characteristic of secular no less than religious developments with other factors which sprang from the heart of Christian Faith and were germinated within the Christian Movement itself. It was an Age when the Western World was marked by the loosing of titanic and seemingly inexhaustible energies. These energies poured through varied channels in many directions. They set some men to plumbing the mysteries of nature; hence the scientific movement with its immense fruitage both theoretical and practical. Others found their minds drawn toward a new disclosure and interpretation of mankind's past; hence the historical movement which altered the intellectual perspective of the world of learning. Similar incentives moved others along more practical lines. Some set themselves to employ the discoveries of science in the creation of a new technology. Others moved out across the face of the earth in political and economic enterprise to bring the resources and peoples of the world into the service of the emerging technical civilization of the West. Above all, the spirit of the times—its discoveries and inventions, its conquests and possibilities—bred an immense confidence in the powers of man, that is of Western man, and an assured assumption of his "manifest destiny" for the rule and liberation of mankind which appeared amply justified by concrete accomplishment.

Christians were children of that age. Inevitably they bore its most characteristic imprints upon them. Three of its features especially contributed to the spread of Christianity—consciousness of the whole world and some acquaintance with its actualities, the practical instrumentalities of expansion, a sense of mission toward all mankind. But in each case, influences from the secular world accentuated rather than created their distinctive Christian expression; each of these features was deeply rooted in the Christian consciousness long before the emergence of the Modern World, indeed from the earliest origins of the Christian Movement.

Christian faith is intrinsically universalistic; that battle had been fought to triumphant conclusion in its first decades; it had always looked out toward all mankind, and through the centuries had followed when it had not preceded the successive advances of explorers and adventurers. While Christianity was able to utilize the instrumentalities made available by the Modern Age, it had sought the same goals long before those instrumentalities were anticipated.

Christianity is also intrinsically missionary, always taking with earnest literalness its commission to "go to all nations." Moreover, the vision and energies which Christianity shared with secular enterprises derived less from the spirit of the times than from its own creative genius. Religion is, as Professor Hocking has so convincingly demonstrated, inherently creative. When vital, it is forever giving birth to new movements and impelling its devotees forth upon new adventures of the spirit and new crusades for human emancipation. In particular, a principal secret of Christianity's record in the recent past is to be found in a series of spiritual renewals and their aftermaths—the Pietistic Movement of the early eighteenth century, the Wesleyan revival toward its close, the missionary impulses which made bold in the first years of the nineteenth century to launch new and daring programs for the evangelization of the world at the very hour of Christianity's threatened eclipse, and, finally, near its end another spiritual resurgence inspired by those two extraordinary colleagues, Dwight L. Moody and Henry Drummond. Here, always, are the true source-springs of Christianity on the march.

In what follows, we shall be primarily concerned with Christian thought and its interrelations with the intellectual trends of the time. But our account will lose perspective unless it keeps constantly in view developments of the Christian Movement in its reaction to and impact upon civilization in the century.

IV

In broad generalization, the sixteenth century was a period of religious revival and reformation, the seventeenth of theological and ecclesiastical consolidation and controversy, the eighteenth of theological disintegration and religious sterility, the nineteenth of spiritual revitalization and theological reconstruction.

On the threshold of this new epoch stands by common acknowledgement the most formative intellect of the Modern Period. It is a truism that any discussion of nineteenth-century thought, whether philosophical or theological, must make its start from Immanuel Kant. Completing his work just as the century was dawning, he bequeathed the issues, and the terms for their discussion, which have largely dominated intellectual controversy since.

There is no more familiar figure in the annals of thought than that of the strange little German scholar whose travels in a long life of eighty years never carried him farther than fifty miles from his native town of Königsberg, whose ordered existence was so methodical that his fellow-citizens were reputed to set their clocks as he passed on his daily stroll, whose sole intimate companion was a faithful male servant.

From this it must not be inferred that Kant was either a provincial in interests or a recluse in spirit. It was his conviction that one need not travel in order to know the world. He read books of history and travel avidly and the metaphysician who had never been fifty miles from home taught physical geography. No man of his time followed with keener attention the events of the day—the course of the French and American Revolutions as well as political developments within Germany. And, as an invariable feature of each day's regimen, he entertained at lunch from two to five friends, never fewer, never more, with whom he spent the early afternoon in sociable discussion.

No one can appraise the thinking of this great little man and his importance for us without some understanding of the forces which moulded his mind. Like all constructive thinkers, even the most original, Kant's convictions developed directly against a background of the dominant intellectual issues of his day, and they cannot be properly grasped without reference to the contemporary situation. Of these formative influences, three are of first importance:

1. Kant's home—its simple, intense, conservative, highly emotional Pietism. This was the atmosphere in which his early impressionable years were passed; and he never wholly escaped from its imprint. Its final influence upon him was twofold. On the one hand, it bred in him a deep-rooted distrust of emotion in religion and a rather parochial blindness to the importance of religious institutions. Kant's religion was moralistic and practical; and it was intensely personal. On the other hand, it bequeathed to him a profound ethical consciousness and a sense for true personal character. Pietism was the source of all that was deepest, most intuitive, least consciously rational in Kant's thought. From it sprang most of his

great constructive convictions—the primacy of moral issues, the command of the categorical imperative, the reality of human freedom and ethical responsibility.

2. The immediate training ground of Kant's philosophical views was the Rationalism of Leibnitz. Its central position may be summarized as follows: If we would discover any significant truth, we must begin by examining the powers of the human mind itself. The proper starting-point for philosophy is not with sense-experience of the external world as Science would propose but with an analysis of our own thinking. By self-examination the mind brings to light the conditions which make our experience of the external world possible. Then it may go further and discover through itself the nature of ultimate reality. It has been truly said that "Kant was a rationalist by education, temperament and conviction." The agony of his own mental struggle was to determine the validity of reasoning; and although the most important outcome of his intellectual labors was to demonstrate the very limited knowledge which is possible for the human mind, he remained at heart a rationalist. His philosophy in one aspect is a rationalistic criticism of the powers of reason.

3. The most determinative impacts upon Kant's mind struck him from two quite different sources—the scepticism of the Scotsman Hume, and the scientific principles of Newton. Despite their contrast these two factors are mentioned together. The former shattered Kant's confidence in the philosophical tradition in which he had been schooled, while the latter attracted him as a dependable substitute. Hume cast doubt on the validity of the whole rationalistic approach; the thought of Newton suggested that in the method of Science rather than in an analysis of human reasoning was to be found the most valid road to truth. Thus Kant's great problem was set for him. Can the mind achieve any valid knowledge whatsoever? If so, how? And of what? How significant is that knowledge when obtained? Most of Kant's reflection moved strictly within the ambit of these questions. Its limitations as well as its great contributions were predetermined by the terms in which his inquiry was defined—terms which Kant inherited from his predecessors.

We can barely touch the fringes of Kant's thought. Our attention must be strictly confined to those two features of it which have most influenced the development of modern theology—his view of the kinds of knowledge which are possible for the human mind, and how they may be attained; and his positive argument for God.

1. We have just noted the context in which Kant's fundamental problem was presented to him. His thought was torn between Rationalism's unbounded faith in the powers of human reason to discover truth, and Scepticism's doubt of the ability of reason to achieve any absolute knowledge. And, as the most promising release from this dilemma, he was attracted to the method of Science. Kant's solution was to set a sharp and impassable gulf between "appearances" and "reality," between things as they seem to us to be and things as they really are, between what he termed the realm of the "phenomenal" and the realm of the "noumenal" or ultimate reality. Concerning things as they appear to be we may through mathematics and physics achieve a kind of knowledge, although it is always knowledge merely of appearances. But of reality, things as they really are, we may never hope to win "knowledge."

The starting-point is the common-sense recognition that the world as it really is comes to each man's consciousness always through the screen of his own mental apparatus; it is "known" only in the framework and under the terms set by that apparatus; therefore such "knowledge" of it as he may possess is forever colored, we might say tainted, by the structure of his own mind. The framework in which reality invariably presents itself for our study is thus discovered to be a set of conditions *within* the mind; of the existence of these conditions apart from the mind which knows, that is, in reality itself, we may never be sure. Indeed of the true character of that reality, our understanding must always be by inference; it may never possess the authority of "knowledge." [5] "Knowledge" of a kind we

5. "The principles which lie at the basis of our knowledge are . . . conditions of *sense*-experience, and that means of our knowledge of appearances, never legitimately applicable in the deciphering of ultimate reality. They are valid within the realm of experience, useless for the construction of a metaphysical

do have. But it is simply the mind's organization of the great wealth of appearances. It is precisely such knowledge which Science aims to develop.

A simple example taken from our familiar experience of the physical world will illustrate the point—my knowledge of a table. On reflection it is obvious that such knowledge of the table as I possess is really only knowledge of the table as it appears to my senses, and to yours. For example, the table is known to me as an object in space and in time. But what assurance have I that the thing itself really exists in a space-time continuum, that space and time are not merely characteristics which our minds impose on the external reality? To be sure, it is a conclusion supported by the identical experience of vast numbers of people; but a *consensus gentium,* no matter how weighty, can never furnish absolute knowledge. The task of verifying the true color of the table is, as we all know, even more difficult. And when we try to pierce through to whatever mysterious and ultimate reality may lie behind the table and my knowledge of it and myself, the veil is even more impenetrable. I can never get entirely beyond my impressions and those of others—how it appears to us—to the true reality of the thing. *That* it is, I know; *what* it is, I can never be sure.

Now, if I may gain no genuine knowledge of a physical object like a table, it is manifest that I have no knowledge of the external world at all, or of other persons; strictly speaking, I have no objective knowledge of myself. Here we touch the crux of the whole matter, and the point at which Kant's thought makes contact with the problems of our own day and becomes vitally important for us. All hinges on what Kant means by "knowledge," and what he means by his favorite word of contrast, "faith." To neither does he give the meaning which our habitual speech attaches to them. In Kant's usage, *knowledge* is rigidly restricted to the interpretation of a limited field of sense-experience—such sense-experience as can be handled by scientific methods; yes, as Kant saw it, such sense-experience as can be handled by the mathematical-physical sciences. There is thus excluded by definition from the scope of possible knowledge all

theory of things in themselves." Norman Kemp Smith, *A Commentary to Kant's Critique of Pure Reason,* Macmillan, 1918, p. xxxv.

æsthetic, all religious, all distinctively personal and individual experience, even all data of the organic realm; in brief, the major part of all that is significant for human life. After the same fashion, *faith* is employed by Kant with a far broader range of meaning than in colloquial use. Since we are forever debarred from "knowledge" in wide areas of experience, our working relationship to them must be in terms of some other attitude than that of "knowledge." That attitude Kant defines as "faith." Thus it will be seen that for him faith is at a far remove from the Sunday School lad's definition of faith as "believing what you know ain't true." Or even from what the New Testament frequently means by faith—the willingness of the human spirit to hazard itself on beliefs felt to be true though never fully proven true.[6] Faith deals with far more secure realities than that. A somewhat free but perhaps not unfair rendering of his meaning would suggest that to Kant *faith* is my practical work-a-day relationship to things and people, which validates itself in practice but can never be verified with mathematical finality. Faith then embraces the assumptions I employ every time I speak to a friend; or, for that matter, every time I act on the hypothesis that I myself am and that the world is what it seems to be. Thus all the really important considerations of practical life fall within its province. Of the truth of faith's content I may have satisfactory pragmatic certainty in experience; but such a pragmatic test can never be sufficient for theoretical demonstration. Now we understand more clearly Kant's boast that he had sought "to abolish knowledge in order to make room for faith." [7]

2. Hardly less important in its influence on subsequent religious thought was Kant's famous argument for God. It followed inevitably from his basic dichotomy of appearance and reality. If we are forever debarred from "knowledge" of ultimate reality, then it is clear that we may never have valid "knowledge" of God, of His existence or His character. And, if the "knowledge" which Science achieves is always merely an interpretation

6. *Cp.* Hebrews 11:8, 13; etc.

7. *Critique of Pure Reason,* B xxx.

of the *phenomenal* world, then it is futile to look to Science or to Nature for evidence of God. The cosmological and teleological proofs—arguments from the necessity of a First Cause behind Nature, or from the evidence of design in Nature—are invalid. If we would discover justification for belief in God, we must seek it in the areas of practical life where we move by "faith"—areas where our guide is not theoretical reason but "Practical Reason." Here Kant found evidence which, to his own mind, was abundantly satisfying and convincing. His argument is a difficult one to put briefly; even in its most persuasive statement, it is not very convincing to modern minds. It may be summarized as follows:

> One of the indisputable facts of human experience is the imperious command of conscience, the presence within my consciousness of a sense of moral responsibility, the claim of the moral law (the categorical moral imperative) upon my allegiance. I do not need to be sure of the nature of ultimate reality to know what I ought to do and how I should live. The moral law is written into my being; the moral imperative is a "given" fact of life; it is not deducible from any other fact or from reason; it is unique. It directs that I ought always to do what I discover to be right, irrespective of my own desires or the outcome of my fidelity, without regard to the success of my efforts or the probable consequences to myself. This command is absolute whether there be a God or not. Kant is very insistent upon that point; the categorical imperative possesses its own authority, even if the heavens fall.
>
> But the moral law, no less than the laws of Science, is a law of reason. If the moral law is reasonable, then clearly those men who respond to it and are completely devoted to its commands should achieve their goals; the purposes which the law directs them to serve should actually be realized. Furthermore, in a fully rational world, while good men would never be moved to right action by the knowledge that thereby they would gain happiness, as a matter of fact happiness would accrue to them, and in exact ratio to the quality of their devotion. Clearly, ours is not such a world. Loyal service of the right does not always accomplish its purposes. Satisfaction is not proportionate to devoted effort. Moreover, no one learns com-

> plete obedience to the moral law within this brief span of life. Therefore we must assume the certainty of a future life where character may be perfected and the inequities of earthly experience righted, and the existence of an all-wise and benevolent Deity who guarantees justice.

Thus, for Kant, the existence of God is implied in our fundamental certainty that the world is reasonable. So to say, He is a necessity if reason is to maintain its self-respect. Or, in his own phrase, God is a "postulate of the Practical Reason."

If space permitted, it would be valuable to trace the development of Kant's two convictions from his day to ours. It is hardly an overstatement that the thinking of the nineteenth and the first quarter of the twentieth centuries is a commentary on the problem as he formulated it. The distinction between noumenal and phenomenal is the single point of reference to which all philosophy since has been oriented. Modern thought's great preoccupation has been with the question—what is the relation of the world of appearances to the world of reality? It is inescapably with us still. And some of the strongest theological minds have been absorbed in the attempt to build a proof for God on evidence from man's moral experience.

However, the first of Kant's two great positions has suffered serious reformulation since his phrasing of it. It has traced a development which he little anticipated and, quite probably, would have deplored. More and more, the distinction has been defined no longer as that of appearances and reality, but of facts and values. Facts, we are told, are the exclusive domain of Science; philosophy and religion are concerned with values. But the modification in the significance of the dichotomy has been even more far-reaching. To Kant it was the distinction between the realm of phenomenal appearances of which we may have "scientific knowledge" but no certainty, and the realm of reality of which we may have no scientific knowledge but such practical certainty as men may live by. Under the alchemy of modern thought, we now confront the contrast between the world of facts of which Science gives us the only genuine knowledge we may have, and the realm of values which is conceded no validity beyond our own appreciations and feelings. What to Kant was only appearance and therefore of negligible philosophical importance has become for us the basis of the only certainty we possess; what was for Kant the supremely important key to reality—the insights achieved through moral experience—has become for us the insecure realm of subjective valuations. The rôles are reversed. Science, formerly merely the useful interpreter of phenomenal appearances, is now hailed as our sole guide to truth, while the moral consciousness, to Kant our one safe pilot to God, struggles to establish its right to tell us what we ought and ought not to do. We recall that Kant's professed purpose in developing his philosophy was "to abolish knowledge in order to make room for faith." The outcome has been almost exactly the reverse of his intention. That part of human thought to which he gave the high word "knowledge"—the elements in experience fit for scientific treatment—has won increasing reverence as the only proper material for philosophical speculation; and its interpreter, Science, has received increasing recognition as the only sure guide to truth. That part of truth to which, in Kant's view, faith alone could give access has been accorded diminishing metaphysical significance; and our guide thereto, "faith," has become increasingly suspect, tainted with the opprobrium of "wishful thinking." [8] The net deposit from Kant's unhappy dichotomy seems to have been twofold: the conviction that the nature of ultimate reality is forever unknowable; and the impression that it is to Science that we are to look for such dependable knowledge as it lies within man's power to attain.

Mankind's indebtedness to the great little philosopher of Königsberg can hardly be exaggerated. But our concern is with the difficulties which philosophical and theological developments in the modern period have created for Christian belief. In that perspective it is hardly an exaggeration

8. Compare the closely parallel estimate of the Kantian influence in A. S. Pringle-Pattison, *The Idea of God in the Light of Recent Philosophy,* Oxford, 1920, pp. 47ff., especially p. 49.

that the influences which have followed from Kant have strangled and cursed the religious thought of our times. And mainly at three points:

1. *The dualism of appearance and reality.* The dichotomy stands condemned not only because of its unhappy consequences. At its face value it is fundamentally unsound. Human experience knows nothing of facts divorced from values or values unrelated to facts; nor of mere appearances or mere reality. When we view a sunset, we do not see wave-lengths or beauty; we see a beautiful sunset. When we know great men, our acquaintance is not with gland enzymes or courage; but with courageous people. The only facts we ever meet in the great rich deep web of human life are pregnant with meaning. So also we never confront values—whether of truth or of beauty or of character or of love or whatever—save as they come to us embedded in concrete facts and mediated to us through the world of facts. By the same token if, as Kant held, we never succeed in pressing behind appearances to pure reality, nevertheless they are always the appearances of something real. And what reality would we wish to make contact with unless it came to us in the only medium through which we would be able to recognize it, the stuff of our phenomenal life? Facts divorced from values are abstractions from the richness of actual experience, useful for scientific purposes only. Values divorced from facts are abstractions from the concreteness of actual experience, attractive to the imagination only. So sympathetic an interpreter of Kant as Professor Kemp Smith put it thus:

> "Existences and values do not constitute independent orders. They interpenetrate and neither can be adequately dealt with apart from considerations appropriate to the other." [9]

9. Norman Kemp Smith, *A Commentary to Kant's Critique of Pure Reason,* p. lxi. *Cp.* A. E. Taylor, *The Faith of a Moralist,* Macmillan, 1930, Vol. I, pp. 55, 62: "Any such severance falsifies the facts of real life, where existence and value appear always as distinguishable, but always is conjoined. . . . In life as we all live it, *all* is given, facts and valuations together, in an undivided whole. . . .
"What confronts us in actual life is neither facts without value nor values attached to no facts, but fact revealing value, and dependent, for the wealth of its content, on its character as thus revelatory, and values which are realities and

2. The second disservice of the Kantian tradition was implicit in the first. It is the insistence upon building *the argument for God* on the basis of moral experience alone, and *without reference to the evidence from the external world of Nature.*

Here the major blame must fall upon the theologians, notably Ritschl and his school, who pressed this feature of Kant's thought to its ultimate. Moral experience became religious experience. All too frequently religious experience became the uncriticized and unverifiable emotional intuitions of the individual worshipper. "What does it matter what Science may tell us about the world of Nature; do we not meet God in our own hearts, and is that not quite enough?" Just here was a fecund source of the nineteenth century's enmity between Science and Religion, and a ground for the discredit of the theistic position in the thought of intelligent men and women.[10]

Kant himself was too wise completely to embrace such an antithesis. His own deeper insight is revealed in the most famous of his dicta: "Two things induce the soul to reverence—the starry heavens above and the moral law within." [11] His sense for the realities of experience overmastered his too narrow logic. Man is and always will be led to belief in God not merely as a necessity of the moral consciousness or an inference from inner experience, but also by contemplation of Nature, the province of scientific inquiry. Moreover, the starry heavens and the moral law are aspects of a single Ultimate Reality. The conclusions they suggest are not exactly alike but they are not unrelated. Indeed the two aspects of our contact with reality are intimately interrelated and interdependent. Any valid idea of God must satisfy our best interpretation of both types of experience; it must include and harmonize them. Neither man's mind nor his soul can rest satisfied until the former discovers that both Nature and values

not arbitrary fancies, precisely because they are embedded in fact and give it its meaning. To divorce the two would be like trying to separate the sounds of a great symphony from its musical quality."

10. *Cp.* Paul Tillich, *The Religious Situation* (tr. by H. R. Niebuhr), Holt, 1932, pp. 17, 41ff.

11. *Critique of Practical Reason,* Rosenkranz, Vol. VIII, p. 312.

point him to God; and the latter finds through Nature as well as through values a vital experience of God. Our study of the findings of Science and our interpretation of the experience of values should both unmistakably lead us to God. Moreover, in general, they should speak of the same God. For all we wish to know about Him we need every ray of light which each study can offer.

3. There is a third weakness in the Kantian heritage which in its ultimate consequences may be more far-reaching for ill. Even if it be conceded that our experience of values is the principal, if not the only, pathway to God, Kant and his succession were misguided in *interpreting values wholly in terms of morality.*

Surely we do not need to return to Plato for reminder that there are at least three great types of the experience of value and that no final priority can be assigned to any one of them. The voice of the moral consciousness is not our exclusive guide to Reality; we require the experience of all that is lovely as well as all that is good. Further, it is manifest that, through the response of the human spirit to beauty, the Divine Spirit may speak to that of man in a manner utterly different from the voice of conscience. And the insights into the divine nature and purpose and into the ways of the divine commerce with man thus gained are utterly different insights from those given through the deliveries of conscience.

The indictment to be drawn against the narrowly moralistic approach of the great Puritan tradition which has followed from Kant and Ritschl is more compelling still. It fails not merely in that it is incomplete, but in that it almost never leads through to its goal (as, indeed, it never did with Kant himself)—to an experience of a Living God. It pictures man reaching up through ethical striving toward God. Living religion always pictures God vitally active in reaching out toward man. The certainty of God is not a deduction from one's own moral effort; it is a response to a persuasive, impelling Presence beyond. This false perspective (together with the predominance of scientific conceptions already noted) is largely responsible for the sterility of the contemporary layman's religious experience, his loss of the vital sense of the reality of God. He is not certain of a Living God because he has been misled as to where and how he should expect to become aware of God.

A closer attention to the rise of Religion in primitive life might have saved us from this fallacy. Apparently, in the early experience of the race, Religion begins rather as a consciousness of the Numinous, the Wholly Other, than as the recognition of conscience, the Wholly Within. But we need not instance primitive religion. We need only recall from our own experience the birth of religion in the soul of a child. The religion of childhood does not begin in consciousness of duty; it is brought to birth by the gift of love, devotion, sympathy, sacrifice, faith from another—parent, nurse, friend. The God whom children know does not speak through a voice within, but through a person without. And the child's sense of duty, if it is more than reluctant acquiescence in an external rule, is the glad return of the child's soul to the trust, the love, the high expectation of another. Religion begins then not in the awakening to something within myself, but in a spontaneous response to someone outside myself.[12]

What religion is at its first birth in the soul of a child, it continues to be in its final maturity. Always its focal reference is definitely beyond me. In terms of its impact upon me, it speaks not through the compulsion of obligation but through the persuasion of love, yes love even to sacrifice. In terms of my response, Religion is not the doing of something because I ought but the gift of self because I must.

V

As we pass from Kant to the nineteenth-century theologians, it will throw light upon our task if we remember the three faculties in the human

12. *Cp.* George Herbert Palmer, *The Autobiography of a Philosopher*, Houghton, Mifflin, 1930, p. 75: "Religion begins, as does love everywhere, with the vision of a person or a cause greater than ourselves, to which, approaching with bowed head, we may give ourselves up regardless of personal gain."

mind posited by traditional psychology—intellect, will and emotion, characterized respectively by thought, volition and feeling. Whatever our judgment upon the faculty psychology, it is a fact of history that, in their approach to religion, men tend to follow one or another of three alternative courses as thought, volition or feeling predominates. Some, of a reflective cast of mind, hunger for understanding; they turn to Religion to query what light it can cast upon the mysteries of human existence; if satisfied in their quest, they discover in Religion ultimate wisdom; their approach is primarily *speculative*. Others, of practical bent and active spirit, seek moral direction and empowerment; they ask not so much what they may believe as how they should live and what they should do; Religion wins them through a commanding claim upon their devotion; their response is mainly *ethical*. Still others yearn for an experience of deliverance from evil which shall unite their souls with the Divine in intimate communication; they desire the assurance of "salvation"; Religion validates itself to their feelings; their interest is *mystical* or *redemptive*. In the history of Christianity, these three types are clearly distinguished in every age from the early Church to our own day. In any period, they furnish one of the most revealing bases of classification of Christian thinkers and one of the deepest causes of division and misunderstanding among Christians. By chance, the three most formative theologians of the nineteenth century, each of whom inherited the legacy of Kant and sought to vindicate Christian Faith afresh against the prevailing scepticism, brought to their task contrasted temperaments and discovered the root of Religion respectively in feeling, in thought and in will. To glance quickly at Schleiermacher, Hegel and Ritschl is to sense the main currents of the century in Christian thought.

The title of Father of Modern Theology belongs, by universal consent, to Friedrich Schleiermacher. "It was not a school that he founded but an epoch." [13]

E. C. Moore is correct in saying, "Of no theologian is it more true that

13. Otto Braun, *Einleitung,* xcix.

we must understand his background, his temperament and his experience if we are to understand his theology." Among the forces which formed his life, three merit mention:

1. The intense *Moravian piety* of his home. The parallel to Kant is striking. There is food for reflection in the fact that Pietism was the nurturing seedplot of the minds of the two most influential thinkers in post-Reformation Christianity. The thought of each may be interpreted in terms of reaction from and return to this original pattern. Kant came to distrust its emotion; Schleiermacher its obscurantism. Kant bore throughout his whole life the impress of its ethical rigor and simple devotion; Schleiermacher of its deep feeling and religious inwardness.

2. *Romanticism.* Kant found escape from the limitations of pietism in the intellectual austerity of Rationalism. Schleiermacher, a half century later, sought refuge from the arid and sterile Deism of the time in lyrical and subjective Romanticism. The opening paragraph of his Soliloquies is a classic expression of the Romantic mood:

> "No choicer gift can any man give to another than his spirit's intimate converse with itself. For this affords the highest boon there is, a clear and undistorted insight into a free being. . . . Come, take the gift, ye who can understand my spirit's thought! May my feelings here intoned be an accompaniment to the melody within yourselves, and may the shock which passes through you at the contact with my spirit, become a quickening impulse in your life." [14]

3. The teaching of *Spinoza,* his pantheism and his vivid sense of the inwardness and immediacy of religious experience.

Our impression of Schleiermacher would be altogether onesided, however, if we thought of him only as philosopher and theologian. His interests and activities extended into a dozen fields. His published writings fill twenty-five volumes. Throughout his career, he was a preacher of rare

14. *Soliloquies* (Eng. trans. of the *Monologen*), p. 9.

brilliance and eloquence. He was an ardent and energetic churchman. His political influence was very considerable. He never surrendered his early artistic interests and associations. Yet to visualize all these public activities is still to see but half the man. The greatest source of his inspiration and his own richest happiness were found through deep and intimate friendships.

> "Everything I do, I like to do in the company of others. Even while engaged in meditation, in contemplation, or in the assimilation of anything new, I need the presence of some loved one, so that the inner event may immediately be communicated, and I may forthwith make my account with the world through the sweet and easy mediation of friendship." [15]

This remained true of his nature, as sensitive as it was powerful, as responsive as it was versatile, all his life through.

The secret of Schleiermacher's originality and of his revolutionary influence upon Christian thought is his insistence upon making *the witness of Christian experience* determinative for both the content and the structure of theology. All rests upon the definition of Religion, and then of Christianity. Religion is defined in the first instance in terms of feeling, "the feeling of absolute dependence upon God." This experience of absolute dependence, which is "an essential element of human nature," leads inevitably through need for fellowship to association with people of like experience and so to the religious community, the Church, and the specific religions. Thus we are brought to the identification of Christianity:

> "Christianity is a monotheistic faith, belonging to the teleological [i.e. active, ethical] type of religion, and is essentially distinguished from other such faiths by the fact that in it *everything is related to the redemption accomplished by Jesus of Nazareth.*" (itals. added)

These preliminary definitions determine the course which the argument must pursue, so different from that of traditional Christian systems. Since

15. *Op. cit.*, p. 37.

Religion at its heart is an experience of dependence, and since the distinctive Christian experience is one of redemption through Christ, the materials for theology are furnished by the inner consciousness of the redeemed person; the task of theology is simply the discovery and disclosure of the inner rationale of that consciousness. The great body of Schleiermacher's *magnum opus, The Christian Faith,* is nothing more nor less than an exhaustive inquiry into the inmost processes of individual Christian life-transformation, and the drawing therefrom of implications regarding God and the world. At first glance, it seems more like a treatise in psychology than in theology. And so, in a sense, it is. Rather, it is a psychological study from which are developed theological corollaries. All of the great themes of faith find treatment. The original feature is that they are discussed as it were incidentally, and always in relation to the central Christian experience.

What, then, is the *experience of redemption* which is determinative for Christian Faith? It is that process through which a human consciousness in which the power of sin is dominant and the awareness of God is dormant is transformed into a consciousness in free and full communion with God. In this changed consciousness, the lower impulses, while still present, are passive and God-consciousness reigns. This substitution in our souls of the rule of the God-consciousness for the present domination of the sensuous consciousness can on no account be achieved by ourselves, but only by Divine Grace. It is accomplished through communication to us of a God-consciousness we do not possess by One in whom that God-consciousness is already perfect. Such a one is Christ. Thus is the unique redemption which distinguishes Christianity from all other religions effected through Jesus of Nazareth.

The inadequacies of Schleiermacher's thought furnish subject-matter for some of the most bitter polemic in present-day Christian discussion. But a man must be judged not alone by his grasp of the full range of Christian Faith, but also by his sense for the distinctive needs of his own day and his capacity to meet them. Here Schleiermacher stands among the greatest. And there is abundant testimony that he saved many contemporaries from unbelief and despair. Moreover, in at least four respects, he impelled modern theology in new directions and framed premises which will force their challenge upon all serious theological inquiry in this and subsequent generations:

1. His insistence that experience precedes theory and must therefore dictate the limits within which theology should work: the basis of the *"theology of religious experience."*
2. His conception of theology as the servant of the Church and the handmaid of preaching.
3. His identification of Christianity as the "religion of redemption through Jesus of Nazareth."
4. His interpretation of the fashion in which Christ effects redemption: the source of modern *"Christo-centric theology."*

VI

To name Hegel is to call up the thought of a highly speculative and a priori schema of *thesis, antithesis* and *synthesis* into which every datum and phase of reality was artificially forced. Such a basic impression is not wholly incorrect. But we miss Hegel's significance and the extraordinary hold of his thought upon men's imaginations unless we appreciate that this schema arose in the first instance from an unusually acute examination of human consciousness. With all the contrast between him and Schleiermacher, they were akin in one fundamental particular: each developed his theology from a profound analysis of the deeper self-consciousness. In this respect, both were prophets of the modern period.

Careful reflection reveals, Hegel pointed out, that at every moment I am more than I appear to be; the self-of-the-moment is organic with its own past and also with its future. Moreover, it is intimately involved with the existence of others, ultimately with all men living and dead and yet to be. Despite this organic unity of experience, however, self-consciousness is inherently plagued by contradiction which can be resolved only by acknowledging the opposites and then reconciling them in a higher synthesis. This, in turn, yields a fresh contradiction leading to a still more ultimate synthesis, and so on endlessly. This process of "dialectic" is "the logic of passion," the very nature of consciousness by which it advances toward self-realization through a sequence of three successive moments—*thesis, antithesis, synthesis.*

This law of development which pervades and dominates all reality finds its highest expression in the history of religious ideas and institutions. Oriental religion, centering all upon the Infinite, finds its antithesis in Greek religion, equally onesided in stressing the finite, while the synthesis comes to realization in the absolute religion of the God-man, of the Incarnation, the Infinite in the form of the finite, i.e. Christianity. In the evolution of the Christian Movement itself, Greek Catholicism with its excessive mysticism and subjectivism stands over against Roman Catholicism with its equally extreme insistence upon the objective authority of law and Church, while the union of opposites in true balance is achieved in Protestantism. A similar development in the history of philosophy finds fulfillment in the Hegelian metaphysic. The sum of the whole matter is that the dialectic of history has been struggling through the ages to issue in those viewpoints which were central to Hegel's own loyalties—the contemporary Prussian state, German liberal Protestantism, Absolute Idealism. It has been suggested facetiously that Hegel might have paraphrased the Pauline dictum, "the whole creation groaneth and travaileth in pain together until now, waiting for the appearance of"—Georg Wilhelm Friedrich Hegel and his philosophy!

It is obvious whither such an analysis of all empirical phenomena—art, politics, philosophy, religion—points. Just as the logic of passion within individual consciousness is discovered to furnish a key to the comprehension of the movement of history, so the inner rationale of all historical development is discerned to be more than a law of progress; history is the process of the self-expression, the self-realization of the immanent Infinite Spirit. History is the coming to consciousness of the Absolute, God. As one writer has put it, "The story of man is the history of God's becoming." Indeed, in his more rigorously logical and self-consistent passages, Hegel does not hesitate to declare that the Absolute knows Himself only through and within human consciousness of Him.

> "God is God only in so far as He knows Himself; His self-knowledge is His self-consciousness in man, is the knowledge man has *of* God, which advances to man's self-knowledge *in* God." [16]

Thus, in Hegel's philosophy Religion takes a central position. More than that, this self-fulfillment of the Absolute which is the very being of history finds consummation in that religion which is the perfect synthesis to all imperfect theses and antitheses, Christianity. Christianity alone achieves the true union of subjective and objective, of Infinite and finite, of spiritual and material, of freedom and law, of mysticism and order. A supreme expression of this fulfillment is the central symbol of Christian Faith—the God-man, the Christ. But it requires little perspicacity to guess which of the great Christian concepts held strongest fascination for Hegel and confirmed him in his predisposition to acknowledge Christianity as the perfect, the final religion. It is the idea of the Trinity. What is the historic dogma of the Trinity but the inspired intuition of that immanental process which is the very secret of Reality? God the Father is pure abstract Idea; God the Son is the eternal going forth of the Infinite into finite being; God the Holy Spirit is the return of the Idea enriched through self-manifestation in incarnation. Thus it was Hegel's avowed intent to vindicate Christianity, indeed, to establish it beyond challenge as true and absolute.

The appeal of this philosophy in its massive symmetry, its all-embracing comprehensiveness, its confident dogmatism, requires no explanation. To the speculatively inclined, its seeming logical coherence and its intellectual assurance offered almost irresistible attraction. To devout believers, the centrality it claimed for Religion and the final authority it appeared to secure for Christianity made winning appeal. But perhaps its strongest hold was upon those who felt their minds slipping toward insecurity and unbelief. At a time of corroding relativism and scepticism, this was a

16. *Encyclopädie*, 565.

Weltanschauung which, in the name of Reason, promised to vindicate the main body of Christian Faith.

The inadequacies of Hegel's rendering of Christianity need not delay us. Apart from its highly abstract and speculative structure, its forced reading of history soon discredited by a more sober scholarship, its dubious rebaptizing of great historic beliefs in the interests of a philosophical system, one feature alone must arouse Christian misgiving—the importance attributed to the idea of the Christ as a symbol, the complete unconcern with the reality of the historical Jesus. Christianity is interpreted as a phase of a world-process rather than as a specific historic religion, the child and fulfiller of Judaism. The reality of Christianity is found in its symbolic embodiment of philosophical *principles* rather than in concrete *deeds* in human history through which the Living, Creator God makes known His Will for man's redemption.

VII

Schleiermacher and Hegel had this in common: both were distinctively "moderns", grateful heirs of humanism. Here Albrecht Ritschl took stand against them both. In intention at least, he was a traditionalist. "Back to the New Testament by way of the Reformation"—this was the motto that guided him steadily. Against every allurement of speculation, Ritschl affirmed that theology should have no traffic with metaphysics: "In dogmatics, one should take up nothing that cannot be used in preaching and in the intercourse of Christians with one another". Against the subjectivism of mysticism, he insisted that Christian theology be anchored in the historical and the concrete—the person of Jesus Christ.

Despite this resolve to cleave to New Testament faith as reclaimed by the Protestant Reformers and to eschew speculative philosophy, in two vital respects Ritschl speaks the language of the theology of his day and thus shows himself its imperfectly emancipated child. The first of these is his insistence upon prefacing theology with epistemology; indeed, his entire theology rests upon a particular theory of knowledge. Over against the Platonists who separate reality from appearances, disdain the latter and encourage man to attempt access to reality via Reason and the mystic path, and over against the Kantians who likewise divide reality from appearances but deny that man can by any route attain unto reality, Ritschl followed Lotze in affirming that we may know reality through its appearances in phenomena. This view supplied the foundation for Ritschl's famous theory that theological affirmations are "judgments of value" based on faith; upon that theory he sought to erect his doctrine of God. "We know God only in His effects upon us. . . . We know the nature of God and Christ only in their worth for us." We know God to be Christlike because of the sovereign impression of Deity made upon us by the disclosure of Him in Jesus. On the other hand, we affirm the deity of Christ because he attests his identity with God to our souls by accomplishing for us the work which God alone can achieve. Beyond these affirmations concerning either God or Christ, Ritschl held it unnecessary and undevout to penetrate.

The second aspect of the influence of then prevailing thought upon Ritschl is to be found in his conception of the nature of Religion. Religion arises, said Ritschl, through vivid agony of inner tension as man knows himself at once a part of Nature and yet, through his spirit, above Nature.

> "In every religion what is sought, with the help of the supernatural power reverenced by man, is a solution of the contradiction in which man finds himself as both a part of nature and a spiritual personality claiming to dominate nature."

Consideration of Christianity, however, brought Ritschl onto less philosophical and more solidly Christian ground. Christianity is the absolutely ethical religion based on the Person and Work of Christ, founder of the Kingdom of God. Here the two interests which dominated Ritschl's attention are linked—the religious interest in personal redemption through Christ and the moral and social interest in the Kingdom of God, "the organization of humanity through action inspired by love." These two he spoke of as two foci about which Christianity revolves as an ellipse.

On the side of redemption, Christ's great gifts to men are two, Justification and Reconciliation,[17] which are found to be virtually identical. Both are mediated through the Church not as a divinely authorized institution but as the *communio sanctorum,* the body of true believers. When thus redeemed through Christ, the Christian enjoys dominion over the world, "the freedom of the Christian man." Christ's supreme ethical significance, however, lies in his vocation as "the historical Founder of Christianity." This vocation was accomplished through the complete moral and religious identity of his "self-end" with God's purpose, the Kingdom of God. The kinship of Christ with his Father is one of ethical purpose.

Even so cursory a sketch of the main outlines of Ritschl's thought must convey an impression of some inconsistency and ambiguity. These followed inevitably from the stance of the writer, with one foot, so to say, in traditional Christian theology and the other in the outlook of his own day. In making his starting-point in epistemology and in defining Religion, he followed the pattern in vogue in then current Theology; on the other hand, in his reading of Christianity, he cleaved to historic faith. Even in his treatment of Christianity, however, ambiguity persisted. In his religious doctrine of redemption, Ritschl was a loyal child of the Reformation. In his doctrine of the Kingdom of God, he broke genuinely new ground; here he was prophetic of some of the most original and powerful developments of the next half century, e.g. the "Social Gospel." Ritschl conceived these two emphases as two foci of an ellipse, but he himself never brought them into organic connection with each other. The ellipse was strained. To press the figure, it tended to break asunder and move as a circle around one or the other focus as a center.

Nevertheless, Ritschl's contribution to subsequent thought was profound and powerful. His polemic against abstruse intellectualism on the one hand and against inchoate aestheticism on the other hand was decisive. His insistence upon the fundamentally ethical character of Christian devotion delivered those who heeded from rationalistic or mystical aberrations. His emphasis upon the Kingdom of God furnished the theological

17. Significantly, this is the title of Ritschl's greatest work.

premise for the social interpretation of Christianity. Most important of all, his unyielding insistence upon Jesus Christ as heart and norm of all that is vital in Christian Faith brought that Faith back to its true center, and gave the generation which was to follow a principle of limitless fecundity. Most of what proved most dynamic and most fruitful in the life of the Church under the leadership of that generation sprang directly from the "recovery" and restoration to centrality of Jesus Christ. This appears clearly in the rise of "Liberal Theology"; and Liberal Theology was the most powerful and important declaration of Christian Faith as the nineteenth century gave way to the twentieth.

INDEX